TOO SOON
TO QUIT

50 WAYS TO
EXPERIENCE
THE BEST
THAT LIFE
HAS TO OFFER

GEORGE SWEETING

MOODY PRESS
CHICAGO

TOO SOON
TO QUIT

This volume is affectionately dedicated to the Trustees of the Moody Bible Institute who are tried and proven partners in reaching this generation with the gospel of Jesus Christ:

Stuart M. Bundy
John Elsen
Robert Erickson
Thomas Fortson Jr.
Richard Gildner
Edward Johnson
Paul Johnson
Roy Nyholm
Bervin Peterson
John Van Der Aa
John Wauteriek
Paul Wills I
and, lastly, to
Joseph Stowell,
my friend and associate.

With warm appreciation,
George Sweeting
Psalm 115:1

Contents

1

Too Soon to Quit

Once, while Francis of Assisi was hoeing his garden, he was asked, "What would you do if you were suddenly told you would die at sunset today?" He replied, "I would *finish* . . . hoeing my garden."

Theologian John Calvin, though plagued by sickness and harassed by his foes, successfully served his generation. Amid enormous opposition, he wrote widely, taught skillfully, and governed Geneva, Switzerland, for twenty-five years. He refused to quit until his work was done.

A woman in Matthew's gospel illustrates the importance of persistence. Though a Gentile, she recognized Jesus as "Lord" and sought His help to heal her daughter. He at first paid no attention to the woman, and His disciples rebuked her. Yet because she was relentless, Jesus rewarded her steadfast faith by healing her daughter (Matthew 15:21–28).

Our perseverance doesn't change God—it changes *us*. Some lessons we will never learn until we are willing to continue . . . even when we feel like quitting. During such times we learn compassion, understanding, and dependability. A good start in life is helpful, but ending well is all-important.

What is faithfulness? Some call it dependability. Others define it as steadfastness. For sure, not enough is being said about hanging in until the job is done . . . about not quitting.

My predecessor at the Moody Bible Institute, William Culbertson, occasionally said his supreme desire was to "end well." It was said of the early Christians on the day of Pentecost, "They continued steadfastly" (Acts 2:42). I like that. It inspires me. In spite of poverty, scarcity, and abuse, they refused to quit.

When Jan Hus was arrested and told that he would be burned to death for his faith, he purposely practiced holding his hand over the fire in preparation for his final test.

On one occasion, Jesus reminded His followers, "No one, having put his hand to the plow, and looking back, is fit for the kingdom of God" (Luke 9:62).

Paul told the Corinthians, "It is required . . . that one be found faithful" (1 Corinthians 4:2). Faithfulness is required, not merely recommended.

Jesus is our ultimate example of not quitting. Even as a child of twelve, He reminded His distraught parents, "Why is it that you sought Me? Did you not know that I *must* be about My Father's business?" (Luke 2:49, italics added). Later, during His public ministry,

He reminded His disciples that His aim was "to do the will of Him who sent Me, and to *finish* His work" (John 4:34, italics added).

Even when Jesus was dying on the cross, He rejected the challenge of the crowd: "Save Yourself, and come down from the cross!" (Mark 15:30). It is so human to let go and quit when under fire. However, it is divine to hang in there. While Jesus was dying, He said, "'It is finished!' And bowing His head, He gave up His spirit" (John 19:30).

I find great encouragement in Paul's words as well: "He who has begun a good work in you will complete it" (Philippians 1:6).

It seems to me that many people are letting go, giving in, and coming down—quitting after ten, twenty, or thirty years. How sad to someday realize that we did not finish our assignment.

Francis Drake once prayed:

> *O Lord, when you give to your servants to endeavor any great matter*
> *Grant us also to know, that it is not the beginning but the*
>   *continuing of the same,*
> *Until it be thoroughly finished, which yields the true glory;*
> *Through Him who, for the finishing of Your work, laid down His life.*

Jesus is our model. It takes great courage to follow His example, and it's not easy. But He has not left us to live in our own strength. God the Father, God the Son, and God the Holy Spirit are available to help us (John 14:16; Philippians 4:13; Jude 24).

This reminds me that God isn't a quitter, and that for me, as well, it is always . . . too soon to quit!

2

An Attitude of Gratitude

It's easy to be grateful when life flows along like we think it should—when the sky is blue, the sun shines brightly, pleasant breezes blow, and a surplus builds in our bank accounts. But what about those times when health wanes and money is scarce? Even during such times of need, a spirit of thankfulness is important because it reminds us of the trustworthy character of God.

The psalmist wrote, "Many . . . are Your wonderful works . . . and Your thoughts which are toward us . . . they are more than can be numbered" (Psalm 40:5). In response, we are challenged: "In *everything* give thanks; for this is the will of God . . . for you" (1 Thessalonians 5:18, italics added). The simple power of a grateful heart is impossible to exaggerate.

An attitude of gratitude encourages a feeling of well-being. Occasionally, I write down the things for which I'm thankful. For example:

- Faith in a caring heavenly Father
- The comfort and direction I receive from reading the Bible
- The love of family and friends
- Health that is reasonably good
- The challenge and enjoyment of work
- The privilege of contributing to the lives of others
- The ability to meet my financial obligations
- A good night's sleep
- Waking up to the smell of coffee and burnt toast (I like burnt toast)
- More than my daily bread to eat
- A daily walk with my wife and a little more coffee
- The privilege of taking our thirteen grandchildren out to breakfast, one at a time, and learning their likes and dislikes
- Fellowship and inspiration with the people of our local church
- Finding a parking place, especially when I'm late
- Laughing enthusiastically until it hurts
- An occasional afternoon nap—"nature's sweet restorative"
- Pruning roses in our garden or picking berries
- Reading a good book
- Listening to old songs . . . and remembering when . . .
- Watching the sun rise and then set at the close of day
- The sound of rain beating on the window pane
- Chatting with neighbors about small things

Especially, I'm thankful for the privilege and pleasure of *prayer*. That, in all the experiences of life, I'm invited to, "by prayer and supplication, with *thanksgiving*, let [my] requests be made known to God" (Philippians 4:6).

Above and beyond everything else, I would join with Paul the apostle in saying, "Thanks be to God"—for what?—"for His indescribable gift!" (2 Corinthians 9:15).

The worst moment for an unbeliever must be when he's really thankful and has no one to personally thank. But for believers, an attitude of gratitude is a solid foundation on which to build our lives.

3

Seldom Repress a
Generous Impulse

Occasionally I recall my Scottish mother, in her lilting brogue, urging her children to "seldom repress a generous impulse." I smile as I think of frugal Scots being encouraged to generosity, yet my mother was sharing a biblical principle. She taught us to cultivate a generous spirit because it is a reflection of the limitless generosity of God.

Mother was not merely passing on a folk saying to her children; rather, she was sharing a biblical principle. She taught us to cultivate a generous spirit because it was a reflection of the limitless generosity of God.

Most of us have been refreshed by the words of the psalmist, "You anoint my head with oil; my cup runs over" (Psalm 23:5). It's the nature of God to give us a full, overflowing cup of goodness and mercy throughout life.

When Solomon was chosen by God to be the king over Israel, he asked the Lord for an understanding heart. God was pleased with his request. In addition to a wise and understanding heart, the Lord also gave Solomon what he did not request: great riches and honor.

The gospel of Luke tells us that the way we give is the way we get, both in this life and the next. "Give, and it will be given to you: good measure, pressed down, shaken together, and running over will be put into your bosom. For with the same measure that you use, it will be measured back to you" (6:38).

A "measure" was a standard, like a quart or gallon. Some merchants gave cautiously, while others were stingy or dishonest. They didn't give beyond measure. Jesus told His disciples that the way people gave was the way they would receive.

I sometimes think of the cross of Christ as a giant plus sign announcing God's infinite, matchless, abounding love for sinners! In John 10:10, Jesus promised His followers abundant life. *Abundant* comes from a Latin word meaning "copious, profuse, and overflowing." It pictures an ocean wave overflowing in every direction. Jesus stated that His purpose in coming was to give us that kind of overflowing life.

The generosity of God motivates us to liberality. Just as the fragrance of a rose clings to the hand of the giver, so a generous spirit is a "sweet-smelling aroma, an acceptable sacrifice, well pleasing to God" (Philippians 4:18).

The early Christians displayed such generous impulses. They faced severe needs as the church expanded. Barnabas sold a field and gave the proceeds to the apostles (Acts 4:36–37). He was generous, not only with his money, but also with his life, as revealed in his decision to give a second chance to young John Mark (15:36–41). Generosity was a trait of the apostolic church, so that Luke could write of the thousands of new believers, "Nor was there anyone among them who lacked" (Acts 4:34). Incredible!

Acts 6 also speaks of another layman who ministered from the overflow of his life. We read that Stephen was full of wisdom, faith, power, and the Holy Spirit. He knew God's generous supply.

Stephen was full of *wisdom*. He was sensitive to the Holy Scriptures. According to Acts 7, he was familiar with the Bible. We, too, could ask, "Am I full of wisdom? Am I growing?"

Stephen was full of *faith*. He knew that "without faith it is impossible to please [God]" (Hebrews 11:6). We begin our spiritual pilgrimage by faith, and we must also continue it by faith.

Stephen was full of *grace*. That word originally spoke of balance, symmetry, and charm. Paul took that word and poured into it the fullness of God's love and redemption for a lost world. Stephen's facial expression even reminded the opposition of an angel. As he was stoned to death, God's abundant supply enabled his face to glow.

Stephen was full of *power*. He lived powerfully, prayed powerfully, preached powerfully, and died powerfully. God's abundance gave Stephen the inner strength to persevere in suffering. His life would have been quite ordinary apart from this infusion of divine power.

Above and beyond all else, Stephen was full of *the Holy Spirit*. His wisdom, faith, grace, and power resulted from the indwelling Holy Spirit, who enabled him to live abundantly.

When we come to the end of life, the question will not be how much we have gotten, but how much we have given. It will not be how much we have saved, but how much we have sacrificed. We are to be producers rather than parasites, givers rather than getters.

In moments of reverie, I can still hear my mother's enchanting voice—echoing my heavenly Father's gentle whisper—challenging me to "seldom repress a generous impulse."

4

Ordinary Ability
When Focused Excels

As a child, Michelangelo told his father, "Deprive me of art and there will not be enough liquid in me to spit." Michelangelo became one of the greatest artists of all time because he knew how to focus with a passion on what was important to him.

A person's ability to focus is like a magnifying glass that directs the rays of the sun with such intensity that they can ignite paper or burn into wood. Paul knew how to focus on essential things: "One thing I do, forgetting those things which are behind and reaching forward to those things which are ahead, I press toward the goal for the prize" (Philippians 3:13–14).

Focusing as Paul did involves several steps. First, we must eliminate as many hindrances as possible. We need to ask ourselves, "Will this help or hinder me in reaching my goal?" The writer of Hebrews

12:1 urged believers to "lay aside every weight." Weights are hindrances that must be discarded.

Second, we must concentrate on our calling. This requires closing the door on anything that subtracts or dims our vision. Paul urged Christians to forget past victories, failures, and sorrows, as they pursued their life's purpose.

Third, we must give our best *now*. Only then will we be ready for what's ahead.

Fourth, we must live each day so as to position and prepare ourselves for what lies ahead.

Fifth, we must press forward daily with a spirit of humility and expectancy.

It is my opinion that we differ little as individuals. While watching the Olympic Games, it was interesting to observe that fractions of seconds separated the greats from the near-greats.

When the storm-tossed disciples on the Sea of Galilee saw Jesus walking on the water, Peter called out, "'Command me to come to You on the water.' . . . But when he saw that the wind was boisterous, he was afraid; and beginning to sink he cried out" (Matthew 14:28–30). As long as Peter focused, he accomplished the impossible. We, too, at times, are called to go beyond the natural, and only a single focus will see us through.

One of the great barriers to focusing is worry. Our English word *worry* comes from the Greek word meaning "to divide the mind." Worry makes us double-minded rather than single-minded. The apostle James warned us that "a double-minded man [is] unstable in all his ways" (James 1:8).

Double-mindedness reminds me of a creature with two heads facing in opposite directions. It's like a rudderless ship, unable to steer and "driven and tossed by the wind" (James 1:6).

D. L. Moody, as a young man, showed no promise of future significance. Concerning his education, writer and teacher Stanley Gundry comments, "The sum of his formal academic training may have been five years . . . and would probably strike those who examined his notes and letters as overly optimistic."

Edward Kimball, Moody's Sunday school teacher, and the one who led Moody to Christ, wrote: "I can truly say . . . that I have seen few persons whose minds were spiritually darker than was his when he came into my Sunday school class. . . . Also, I think the committee of the Mount Vernon Church seldom interviewed an applicant for membership who seemed more unlikely ever to become a Christian . . . still less to fill any sphere of public or extended usefulness."

Moody's life is a vivid illustration of a person of ordinary ability who focused his gifts and excelled. He went on to become a world-famous evangelist as well as the founder of two prestigious schools that continue to this day. Moody would often challenge his audiences by saying, "Give me a person who says, 'This one thing I do,' and not, 'These fifty things I dabble in.'"

There is surely no sight so sublime, no influence so irresistible, no nobility so godlike as a person doing one right thing for the glory of God. Unfortunately, too many of us change our goals so often that progress is impossible. Single-mindedness for a lifetime is awesome to behold.

Jesus encouraged His hearers to focus: "The lamp of the body is the eye. If therefore your eye is good, your whole body will be full of light" (Matthew 6:22). Literally, Jesus was urging us to be "one-eyed" people, or people with one-track minds, because He knew that ordinary ability, when focused, *excels.*

5

Never Give In

Winston Churchill was asked to bring the commencement address to his alma mater, Harrow School. The auditorium was hot and the program long. When Churchill was finally introduced, he approached the podium and spoke twenty-nine words: "Never give in, never give in, never, never, never, never—in nothing, great or small, large or petty—never give in except to convictions of honor and good sense." Needless to say, they never forgot his speech.

Extraordinary faithfulness was a mark of the early Christians. Day after day, month after month, year after year, long after the ascension of Jesus, "they continued steadfastly in the apostles' doctrine and fellowship, in the breaking of bread, and in prayers" (Acts 2:42). They were steadfast . . . reliable . . . they refused to quit.

A requisite for apostolic success was steadfastness. They depended on each other, just as they depended on Jesus. The early Christians were a company of equals committed to the Good News and to one another in spite of the consequences.

When the church in Antioch heard of the famine among those in Jerusalem, they sent Paul and Barnabas with money to buy food for their starving brothers and sisters (Acts 11:27–30). When Dorcas died, the believers at Joppa sent word to Peter to help their sister in the faith. All the widows were standing beside her bed when he arrived. Peter went at their request and raised Dorcas from the dead (Acts 9:36–43).

They were also steadfast in observing the ordinance of Communion. Receiving "the bread" and "the cup" of Communion, according to Scripture, is *not optional.* We're instructed, "*Do this* in remembrance of Me" (1 Corinthians 11:24, italics added). The bread and the cup poignantly underscore our Lord's steadfastness. Luke said, "He steadfastly set His face to go to Jerusalem" (Luke 9:51).

They were also steadfast in prayer. After the ascension of Jesus, His followers returned to the upper room and "*continued* with one accord in prayer" (Acts 1:14, italics added). Prayer influenced every area of their lives. Prayer is the Lord's cure for caving in (Luke 18:1).

Our world today argues *against longevity.* The attention span of many people has been reduced to fifteen-second sound bites. A big appetite exists for a quick fix, the sensational, even the bizarre, with little passion for commitment even unto death.

More recent examples of perseverance can be found in stories of missionaries like John and Betty Stam, who served in China with great success. However, in December 1934, the Communist forces attacked the city where the Stams served. John and Betty were led to a clump of pine trees on a hill outside of town, where John was ordered to kneel. Another quick command was given, a sword flashed, and John was dead. Betty quivered, but only for a moment. With another sword stroke, she and John were united forever in heaven.

As the journalists of the world told their story, thousands of people from many lands volunteered to take their place. Nothing could keep John and Betty from their commitment. They never gave in. They were faithful . . . even to death.

"Let us run the race that is before us and never give up" (Hebrews 12:1 NEW CENTURY).

6

How to Excel

Over my desk hangs a large, colorful poster of an Olympic runner winning a race. Underneath are the words, "Run *in such a way* that you may obtain [the prize]" (1 Corinthians 9:24, italics added). In other words, average running *doesn't win!*

Jesus challenged His followers, "Let your light *so shine* before men . . . and glorify your Father in heaven" (Matthew 5:16, italics added). In essence, Jesus said, "Mediocre shining doesn't glorify God."

Paul and Barnabas "*so spoke* that a great multitude . . . believed" (Acts 14:1, italics added). Passionless speaking convinces no one.

Mediocrity doesn't excel! To make a difference in life we ought to pursue excellence. By excellence I mean that which is choice, first-rate, top-drawer. But you ask, what standard do we use to measure excellence, and where do those standards come from?

John W. Gardner, author and former United States Secretary of Health, Education, and Welfare, said, "Standards are contagious. They spread throughout an organization, a group, or a society. If an organization or group cherishes high standards, the behavior of individuals who enter it is inevitably influenced."

"Similarly," Gardner wrote, "if slovenliness infests a society, it is not easy for a member of that society to remain uninfluenced in his own behavior. With that grim fact in mind, one is bound to look with apprehension on many segments of our national life in which slovenliness has attacked like dry rot, eating away the solid timber."

Just as one quality person encourages others to strive for excellence, so mediocrity spreads like a cancer. The dictionary defines mediocrity as "ordinary, neither good nor bad, barely adequate, poor, inferior."

Mediocrity is like playing five strings on a ten-stringed instrument. Mediocrity is a person with eagle talent never flying more than a few feet off the ground like a prairie chicken. Mediocrity is a person with jet power doing pushcart work. Mediocrity is merely standing and walking when we were created to "mount up with wings like eagles" (Isaiah 40:31). We need to beware of the menace of mediocrity.

Artist Charles Close said, "Art is a profession without a measuring system. There is no way to tell if what I am doing is good. So what is quality? I don't know the answer."

However, the Bible has a lot to say about excellence and gives us standards by which to measure it. Psalm 8:1 proclaims, "O Lord, our Lord, how excellent is *Your name* in all the earth, You who set Your glory above the heavens!" (italics added).

According to the psalmist, *God's name* is the standard of all excellence. His name is symbolic of all that He is. God is holy! God's holiness implies that no one compares with Him. He is also merciful, almighty, just, unchanging, loving, and eternal. God not only exemplifies excellence in His person, but also in His works (Psalm 19:1), His ways (2 Samuel 22:31), and His will (Romans 12:2). He is our standard of excellence.

Some people appear to think that striving for excellence is earthly and carnal. But to the contrary, all excellence originates with God and exists because of God. I began my own pursuit of excellence while a student at the Moody Bible Institute of Chicago. I learned from quality teachers and leaders who visited our campus how to excel for God. They challenged me to *be my best* in every area of life.

However, along the way, I encountered serious roadblocks. During my junior year, the doctors discovered I had cancer. I underwent surgery and a series of radiation treatments. I faced the prospect of not living through that year. But God intervened and spared my life. With the prayers and help of fellow students, I completed the school year with honors and slowly regained my health.

To me, graduating from Moody Bible Institute was just the beginning of my pursuit of Christian excellence.

John W. Gardner was right: "Whoever I am, or whatever I do, some kind of excellence is within my reach." Excellence is not just for a privileged few. It's for me to strive for, and you as well—whoever you are, wherever you are, and whatever you do.

7

The Capacity to Care

I was moved by a newspaper article about a once-lovely countess who had been caged like an animal for forty years in a castle outside Milan, Italy. She had been locked in a dingy room where she slept on rags on the floor, behind walls spattered with her blood.

Finally, at age sixty-five, she was carried on a stretcher from her jail. No longer beautiful, she was an emaciated scarecrow. Her matted gray hair reached down to her thighs. She was little more than skin and bones. She screeched in terror at the sight of her rescuers and babbled disjointed phrases in a dialect nobody understood.

I was also shaken by a small news item about a fourteen-year-old boy who took his own life because "no one seemed to care." He felt no love from anyone, except his dog, and in a brief suicide note written to his parents, he left instructions for *the care of his dog*.

"No one seemed to care." What a rebuke to our lack of compassion—or lack of showing our love. It is likely that the boy's parents did care, but distracted by the demands of everyday living, they failed to communicate their love.

Christianity exploded in the Roman Empire when Christians mirrored the love of Jesus. They announced the gospel through a practical demonstration of love for other people.

David Livingstone, the nineteenth-century missionary to Africa, could not always communicate the Christian message verbally to the people to whom he ministered, but all *felt* the care of his loving heart.

D. L. Moody recounted that not until hearing Henry Moorehouse speak on John 3:16 for a solid week did he begin to understand the life-changing power of God's love. Richard Ellsworth Day, in his biography *Bush Aglow,* recorded Moody's account of what happened to him at those meetings: "I never knew up to that time that God loved us so much. This heart of mine began to thaw out; I could not keep back the tears. I just drank it in. . . . I tell you there is one thing that draws above everything else in the world and that is love."

It's one thing to know that God's love is the greatest of all gifts, but it's quite another thing to live life in light of that knowledge. Moody described the amazing result of his study of God's love:

I took up that word "love," and I do not know how many weeks I spent studying the passages in which it occurs, 'till at last I could not help loving people. You take up the subject of love in the Bible! You will get so full of it that all you have got to do is to open your lips, and a flood of the Love of God flows out.

34

After this happened, Moody, who was already a successful Christian worker, saw for the first time the secret of a winsome church:

> The churches would soon be filled if outsiders could find that people in them loved them when they came. This . . . draws sinners! We must win them to us first, then we can win them to Christ. We must get the people to love us, and then turn them over to Christ.

Moody was empty and frustrated before he experienced the power of God's love in his life. His congregations even showed signs of falling away. He found himself wondering if the gospel might need something added to it to make it attractive to people.

While reading on a train from California after attending a Sunday school convention, Moody recalled Henry Moorehouse saying to him four years earlier, "You are sailing on the wrong track. If you will change your course, and learn to share God's words instead of your own, He will make you a great power."

That summer Moody made a commitment to give even his ignorance to God, and new life flooded his life and his church. Even the August heat couldn't keep the people away.

At the close of his Chicago church ministry and before becoming world famous, he told his successor, Dr. William J. Erdman, "Give the people *the importance of love.* If they are right here, they will be right 95 percent of the time."

It's one thing to know that God's love is the greatest of all gifts; it's quite another thing to live life in light of that knowledge. Yet the capacity to care is what makes life worth living.

8

A Good "Forgettory"

A good "forgettory" is as important as a good memory.

For the most part, we tend to remember the happy occasions of life. Memory consciously and unconsciously tries to bury the painful experiences of life. But sometimes the memories of the past won't go away. At those times, trying to forget . . . isn't enough!

I spoke to a friend who was haunted by past failure. I compared her obsession with the past to touching a door that is wet with red paint. By visiting and remembering her failures, she was staining the present with the memories of the past.

Wistfully, she reminded me that "forgetting" is more difficult than just quoting a phrase of Scripture. I agreed, and then offered these ideas to help her forget:

1. *Make everything right that needs to be made right.* Face known sin, deal with it, and repent. Repentance and restitution begin the forgetting process; it is difficult to forget wrongs until they are made right. An accusing conscience keeps memory frightfully alive.

It's helpful to read Psalm 51 and pray, with David, "Wash me . . . from my iniquity" (v. 2). "Purge me with hyssop, and I shall be clean; wash me, and I shall be whiter than snow" (v. 7). "Create in me a clean heart, O God, and renew a steadfast spirit within me" (v. 10). "Restore to me the joy of Your salvation" (v. 12).

David's life was not free from sin, yet he was called "a man after [God's] own heart" (1 Samuel 13:14) because of his wholehearted repentance. Upon receiving God's forgiveness, we can forget the things that are behind (Philippians 3:13).

2. *Reverse the process of memory.* Memory is helped by repetition. Therefore, we cannot spend time reliving our past and still forget. We may sincerely repent and forsake our sins and yet continually revisit them. In moments of defeat, we may even encourage and relish those memories. This process makes forgetting very difficult.

Most painful experiences in life beg to be forgotten. In learning to forget, we should work *with* nature, rather than *against* it.

3. *Displace the thoughts of past sin with greater thoughts of God's unlimited grace.* In contemplating the cross of Jesus and His sacrificial death, we experience powerful, life-changing grace. God's love is greater than anything and everything we have done or failed to do.

The Bible exhausts the possibilities of language in telling us how completely God forgives us when we come to Him in repentance and faith: "As far as the east is from the west, so far has He removed our transgressions from us" (Psalm 103:12; see also Isaiah 44:22; Micah 7:19).

Scripture promises that when God forgives, He also forgets. "Their sin I will remember no more" (Jeremiah 31:34). Since God forgives and forgets . . . who are we to remember?

A good "forgettory" is as important as a good memory.

9

Do You Feel
Like Quitting Today?

On a regular basis I receive mail from radio friends who feel like quitting. Sometimes the cause is difficulty in marriage or restless children, unpleasant working conditions or poor health. It's not so much about giving up on the faith as giving up on the experiences of life. "I can't make it work." "I'm trapped in a whirlpool of debt." "All seems futile. I can't go on."

Each of us at some point in life has experienced moments of doubt, feelings of inadequacy, even failure, possibly deep financial needs or physical pain. At times we've even thought the price was too great: Maybe I should quit . . . this isn't for me!

Job, of the Old Testament, must have felt that way, too. Actually, Job was the very best man God could find during his lifetime. The Lord said of Job, "There is none like him on the earth, a blameless and upright man, one who fears God and shuns evil" (Job 1:8; 2:3).

And yet, in the depths of his trials, Job cursed the day of his birth and questioned, "Why did I not die at birth? Why did I not perish when I came from the womb?" (3:11). Job felt so bad and so overwhelmed that he loathed life (see 10:1). In his despair, he questioned, "Show me *why* You contend with me" (v. 2, italics added); and in confusion and pain he cried, "Cease! Leave me alone" (v. 20). Job despaired of life itself. Job felt like quitting!

Why do we feel like quitting? Perhaps it's because we lose sight of two important facts. The first fact is that *God loves us* . . . in spite of everything. In our trials we're sometimes a contradiction even to ourselves, and yet God still *loves us.* Scripture affirms repeatedly that, come what may, God loves me and deeply cares for me (Matthew 10:28–31; 1 Peter 5:7).

Second, we need to remember that God can be fully trusted. Job never knew why he suffered so severely. We know, because we have the revelation of Scripture that tells us why he suffered. Job was actually God's illustration to Satan of a good and godly man who fully trusted amid desperate circumstances (Job 1:8–12). It's true that Job said some foolish things; however, he refused to quit, and ultimately "the Lord restored Job's losses *when* he prayed for his friends" (42:10, italics added). Prayer has a boomerang effect!

What should I do when I feel that I can't go on? Should I quit? No! Never! Rather, hang on to these two absolutes: *God loves me* and *God can be trusted.* He is *too wise* to make a mistake and *too loving* to be unkind. I find great encouragement in the words of Paul: "We are hard pressed on every side, yet not crushed; we are perplexed, but not in despair; persecuted, but not forsaken; struck down, but not destroyed" (2 Corinthians 4:8–9).

Remember . . . it's *always* . . . too soon to quit!

1 0

I'm Sorry; I'm Wrong

A California company called Apology Accepted has built a business out of people's conflicts. According to *People* magazine, they will tailor-make an apology to fit any occasion. The owners, who call themselves "locksmiths who reopen the doors of communication," will provide "whatever it takes, from a box of chocolates to a yacht," to resolve and rebuild broken relationships.

The words "I'm sorry; I'm wrong" are life building. They can make a difference in our relationships with family, friends, and people in general.

A staff member unintentionally offended another employee. The situation grew tense and awkward. I urged my friend to go to the offended person and sincerely apologize. When he did, the tension broke and a solid friendship began to build.

"I'm sorry; I'm wrong," earnestly spoken, can build relationships.

Yet many people seldom apologize, possibly because they are afraid to admit error or weakness. However, a willingness to apologize is a characteristic of strength. Such honesty tells others that we recognize our humanness and know that God isn't finished with us yet. It also acknowledges that we are still in the process of being conformed to the image of Christ.

Some time ago, my wife and I were driving from a family conference ground in Speculator, New York, to another conference in Schroon Lake, New York. My wife was sure of the road to take; however, I knew a shortcut. After driving many miles in the wrong direction, I realized I was hopelessly lost. With a sheepish grin, I confessed, "I'm sorry; I'm wr-wr-wr-wrong."

The word *confession* comes from two Greek words, *homo* and *legeo,* which combined literally mean "to say or speak the same thing." Confession means "to agree with God," "to say what God has already said." Primarily, it is "to agree with God" concerning our individual sinfulness, but it is also to agree with God concerning Jesus, God's only provision for our sins.

Scripture tells us that David was a man after God's own heart. Evidence of this is seen in his wholehearted repentance after his sin. For a time, David *disagreed* with God and willfully rebelled. However, in Psalm 51, he poured out his soul in full agreement with God.

"Wash *me* thoroughly from *my* iniquity, and cleanse *me* from *my* sin. For I acknowledge my transgressions, and my sin is ever before me" (vv. 2–3, italics added; see also vv. 7, 10, 12–13).

David's confession was very personal. He prayed, "Wash *me* thoroughly from *my* iniquity, and cleanse *me* from *my* sin."

The words "I'm sorry; I'm wrong" are equally helpful to the follower of Christ in our practical everyday living. The Old Testament prophet Amos asked, "Can two walk together, unless they are agreed?" (Amos 3:3). The obvious answer is no. To agree with God is essential to walking with God.

It's a good practice to start each day with a time of honest confession to God. This is the path to building and maintaining a strong, vital relationship with Him. However, if we're in the habit of confessing our failures to God, we will find it much easier to confess our faults to one another.

"I'm sorry; I'm wrong" is more than a catchy phrase. When spoken with heartfelt sincerity, it becomes a liberating attitude that establishes a solid life.

1 1

The Caleb Secret

What do you do when you're trying to remain optimistic but are surrounded by a bunch of pessimists? Perhaps we can learn from the example of a famous Old Testament optimist named Caleb.

After four hundred years of slavery, the Jewish people were delivered from Egypt. Sustained by faith, they overcame captivity, the Red Sea, and the wilderness to face their biggest challenge—*possessing the land of Canaan.*

In preparation, twelve spies searched the land and agreed that it flowed "with milk and honey" (Numbers 13:27). But ten of the spies also argued that the cities were "fortified and very large" (v. 28) and the people like "giants" (v. 33).

There was truth in what they said because the inhabitants wouldn't give up without a fight. The negative report of the majority caused pandemonium among the people so that they "wept that night" (14:1) and spoke of mutiny against Moses (v. 4).

In direct contrast, *the minority report* of Caleb and Joshua throbbed with faith. They urged the people, "Go up at once and take possession, for we are well able to overcome it" (13:30).

What made the difference? They described the same land, except that Caleb and Joshua concentrated on God's ability while the ten were consumed by their own inability. The difference was their relationship to God (14:8–9).

The attitude of the ten minimized their vision of themselves. "We were like grasshoppers in our own sight, and so we were in their sight" (13:33).

This grasshopper complex resulted from focusing on the opposition rather than God. That's always how it is when we focus only on our problems. The obstacles loom beyond reason.

Though they felt like grasshoppers, they were really God's chosen people. God had vanquished Egypt for their sakes and defeated Amalek and all who opposed them. Every promise He had kept, but now God's great deeds were forgotten.

Six times in Numbers, Deuteronomy, and Joshua we read that Caleb "wholly followed the Lord." The phrase tells us Caleb's secret. What Caleb *was* determined what Caleb *did*. "But My servant Caleb," God said, "because he has a different spirit in him and has followed Me fully, I will bring into the land where he went, and his descendants shall inherit it" (14:24).

Caleb had a God-believing attitude. His was not a spirit of fear, but of faith. He was an overcomer!

Going against the tribal leaders and the congregation of Israel took courage, but Caleb and Joshua were right—and the majority wrong.

God said, "Possess the land." He said, "It's a gift" (see 13:2). Unbelief said, "We can't." By contrast, Caleb viewed the difficulties as opportunities to display God's power.

Notice Caleb's attitude of humility toward himself. He saw himself as linked to God in a sacred partnership. "If the Lord delights in us," he reasoned, "we'll succeed."

Caleb's secret was simple, yet profound. "He fully followed." His commitment was total. The unbelief of the ten resulted in the world's longest funeral march (14:35).

How is it with you? Are you facing a Kadesh-Barnea that could change the course of your life? It may be a circumstance to accept, a work to be undertaken, or a burden to be borne.

Remember Caleb's secret. Don't be overwhelmed by circumstances or awed by difficulties. They don't matter. It's your attitude toward God—His glory and His will—that really counts. Remember, He can do "exceeding abundantly" above all that you ask or think (Ephesians 3:20).

How shortsighted to fret about obstacles when we're linked with God. Caleb won the battles of life . . . because he first won the battles of faith and commitment. When you stand with God, you may be outnumbered, but you'll never be in the minority.

1 2

Do You Have the Joy?

Through no credit of my own, I was born with a happy disposition. As a child in grade school, I lived on the sunny side of life. I was also a giggler as a child and occasionally was asked to leave the classroom until I could compose myself. Try as I did to be serious, upon my reentering the classroom, most would break into laughter, and I was sent into the hallway again. I've learned since, however, that Christian joy has little to do with external brightness based on human disposition. True authentic joy is a by-product of a right relationship with God, so it can exist even in the presence of intense persecution (James 1:2–3).

Though there is no scriptural record of Jesus laughing, joy characterized His life. Repeatedly Jesus spoke of joy, gladness, and rejoicing. Even as He approached the Garden of Gethsemane, Jesus reminded His disciples, "These things I have spoken to you, that *My joy* may remain in you, and that *your joy* may be full" (John 15:11, italics added)

Centuries before, the birth of Jesus had been foretold—that He would be anointed "with the oil of gladness *more than* [His] companions" (Psalm 45:7, italics added). Added to that is the fact that Jesus possessed the Spirit of God fully, which guaranteed Him joy as part of the fruit of the Spirit (Galatians 5:22). Jesus must have been the most joyful person who ever lived.

Probably because the Gospels tell us that "Jesus wept" and Isaiah referred to Him as "a man of sorrows," we tend to forget the joyfulness of Jesus. Matthew celebrated his conversion with a party (Luke 5:29), and Jesus joyfully shared, earning Himself some unsavory charges (Matthew 11:19).

Jesus performed His first miracle at a wedding party (John 2:1–10), probably to save the bride and groom from embarrassment.

In the parables of the lost sheep, the lost coin, and the lost son (Luke 15), there was "great joy" when the lost was found. The father of the Prodigal Son rebuked the older brother, saying, "It was right that we should *make merry and be glad*" (Luke 15:32, italics added).

Repeatedly Jesus directly and indirectly called for joy. At least three times He commanded, "Be of good cheer." Often, He said, "Fear not," or "Peace be to you." Many times He said, "Blessed are you," which really means "Happy are you."

After the Samaritan woman met Jesus, she was so overjoyed she forgot her water jar and rushed back to town to tell her friends about Jesus (John 4:28). After Zacchaeus met Jesus, he received Him into his home "joyfully" (Luke 19:6).

The night before Jesus was crucified, after instituting the Last Supper, He sang a hymn with His disciples (Matthew 26:30). Though things looked dark, Jesus maintained His joy.

His cousin and forerunner, John the Baptist, had been beheaded; the crowds had dwindled; His brothers had turned against Him; soon His disciples would forsake Him and flee. Then He would be arrested, scourged, mocked, and crucified.

Yet, Jesus told His disciples not only of *His own joy,* but also of the *fullness of joy* no one could take from them: "You now have sorrow; but I will see you again and your heart will *rejoice,* and your joy no one will take from you" (John 16:22, italics added).

Jesus, who is called "a man of sorrows" in the Scriptures, also left us *a legacy of joy.* And our future includes a mega-celebration greater than any our world has known. It will be the biggest, brightest party of all, called "the marriage supper of the Lamb" (Revelation 19:9). About it, John writes, "Let us be *glad* and rejoice and give Him glory" (v. 7, italics added).

1 3

Lessons from the Spider

Robert the Bruce became king of Scotland in 1306. Scotland was at war with England—and not doing too well. Legend tells how Robert once took refuge in a cave to hide from the armies of England. While lying on a bed half dozing, he saw a spider trying to attach its web to a ceiling beam. Time after time, it tried and failed. However, on the seventh try, the spider succeeded.

A series of battles followed, climaxing in the Battle of Bannockburn in 1314. It was there where Scotland won its independence, and Robert the Bruce became Scotland's folk hero.

The lesson of the spider is captured in the maxim, "If at first you don't succeed, try, try again." It is always . . . too soon to quit. We dare not allow the failures of today to impede our progress tomorrow. As Christians, we have numerous examples who demonstrated the power of perseverance:

Jeremiah tells of a potter who made a clay vessel that was marred (Jeremiah 18:4), so he made it again—until it was the way he wanted it to be.

Moses, who was faithful in so many things, failed greatly in Kadesh, in the Wilderness of Zin. There was no water for the people, and they were worried and complaining. The Lord asked Moses to "speak to the rock before their eyes, and it will yield its water . . . [to] give drink to the congregation and their animals" (Numbers 20:8). Moses did not follow this command but instead "lifted his hand and struck the rock twice with his rod" (v. 11). The Lord *did* provide the water as promised, but because of his disobedience Moses was not allowed to bring the people into the land which the Lord had given them. Yet God did not give up on Moses. He allowed Moses to lead the people up to the very threshold of the Promised Land, and Jesus Himself praised the witness of Moses.

The Lord told Jonah to "go to Nineveh . . . and cry out against it; for their wickedness has come up before Me" (Jonah 1:2). Jonah was disobedient and traveled as far away from Nineveh as he could. But God recommissioned Jonah (3:2) and Nineveh was given a second chance (vv. 5–10).

Peter denied the Lord three times in the courtyard of the high priest's mansion (Matthew 26:69–75), yet he found forgiveness and continued on to become the leader of the twelve disciples.

John Mark left Paul and Barnabas during the middle of the first missionary journey when the party had only reached Pamphylia (Acts 13:13; 15:38). This disappointed Paul to the extent that later he refused to let Mark go with him on a missionary trip. The contention between Paul and Barnabas over this matter was so great that the two parted company. Yet Barnabas gave Mark another chance (15:39), and John Mark eventually was given the remarkable honor of writing the second gospel of the New Testament.

Paul's preconversion days were utterly disappointing. He consented to the murder of Stephen (Acts 7:58). He led waves of attacks against the early Christians (8:3). Yet, one day, his life was transformed by Jesus, and he became a new person . . . old things passed away.

Later Paul wrote, "Forgetting those things which are behind and reaching forward to those things which are ahead" (Philippians 3:13).

Maybe you, like Robert the Bruce, are in your cave of defeat. You, too, need to look up for wisdom and renewed strength, for God's mercies are new every morning. Remember the lesson from the spider. "If at first you don't succeed . . . try, try again." But most of all, remember the lesson from the lives of Moses, Jonah, Peter, John Mark, and Paul. As long as we are alive, God is the God . . . of the second, third, and fourth chance.

1 4

Living at Flood Tide

How many times have you heard someone question the meaning of life as he or she looked back across a lifetime? Even many Christians confess to not enjoying the quality of life they believe God intends for His children. Yet in spite of the spiritual dryness we may feel, we can learn to live at flood tide in this life as we abide in Christ and apply His Word.

God's intentions for us are expressed in words and phrases such as *victory, abundant, overcome,* and *more than conquerors* (Romans 8:37). The very purpose of the coming of Jesus was that we might experience life "more abundantly" (John 10:10). The word *abundant* suggests a sea wave splashing in every direction . . . water in a teeming supply.

Stephen lived at flood tide. His name means "crowned." Stephen was a God-crowned follower of Jesus.

Because of the explosive growth of the original church, Stephen was among those chosen to do the work of a deacon, allowing the apostles to give themselves "to prayer and . . . the word" (Acts 6:4). Luke credits Stephen with being "full of the Holy Spirit and wisdom" (v. 3), "full of faith" (vv. 5, 8), and "full . . . of power" (v. 8).

Being filled with God transformed Stephen. Some imagine that the fullness of the Spirit of God pertains to a single facet of life, whereas the biblical concept includes the whole of life.

By the phrase *fullness of the Holy Spirit,* I mean the control of the Holy Spirit. This is the key to living a life at flood tide.

For some, the fullness of the Spirit is a crisis experience, though it doesn't have to be. In studying the life of D. L. Moody, we find his early success could be attributed to human enthusiasm and personal magnetism.

Writing to Charles Blanchard of Wheaton College, Moody's co-worker Emma Dryer described Moody as "a divinely equipped flying artillery on life's battlefield."

Though never ordained and lacking formal education, Moody built the largest Sunday school in America before he was twenty-seven. He also founded the Illinois Street Church while serving as director of the Chicago YMCA.

As his responsibilities grew, Moody realized how unprepared he was for God's call on his life. His inadequacy led to great personal dissatisfaction and even despair.

After he spoke at a Sunday school service in New York, an elderly man cautioned Moody, "Young man, when you speak again, honor the Holy Spirit." Moody could not forget his words. Several months later, two women, Mrs. Sarah Annie Cook and Mrs. Hauxhurst, reminded him of their prayers on his behalf for spiritual power. Though annoyed with them at first, he soon acknowledged his deep need for God's power for service.

The catastrophe of the 1871 Chicago fire added to his desperation. While he was visiting Philadelphia, New York, and Boston to raise money to rebuild the burned-out Chicago ministries, the crisis deepened. Continually, he called on God to fill him.

In the process, God redirected Moody from his Chicago ministries to the work of an international evangelist. While walking down a street in New York City, Moody yielded himself to the will of God. He was so overcome by this experience that he sought the home of a friend to give himself to meditation and prayer. There, alone with God, Moody yielded his life to the Holy Spirit. "I can only say that God revealed Himself to me, and I had such an experience of His love that I asked Him to stay His hand."

Moody's dry spell was over, and he began to live at flood tide. "I was all the time tugging and carrying water," said Moody, "but now I have a river that carries me."

What God did for Stephen and Moody, He's able to do for you. When you experience the fullness of God, you'll never again need to question the meaning of life.

1 5

The Call to a Holy Life

Leonard Ravenhill once observed, "The greatest miracle that God can do today, is to take an unholy man out of an unholy world and make him holy, and then put him back in that unholy world, and keep him there."

Peter and John were, without doubt, holy men. In Acts 3, they healed a lame beggar in the name of Jesus, resulting in immediate popularity. When Peter told the people that the beggar was healed through the power of Jesus, a crisis erupted that confounded the Sadducees and other religious leaders. They took the two disciples into custody and brought them before the high priest for public questioning.

By calling attention to Jesus, the disciples cut the thin skin of their interrogators. The Sadducees rejected any possibility of a resurrection, while the priests only a few weeks earlier had shared in crucifying Jesus. Any talk of resurrection and healing in Jesus' name was the last thing they wanted to hear.

The proof of a miracle, however, was undeniable. A man who had been lame for more than forty years was walking among them.

What was it that gave Peter and John such prominence on this occasion? How is it that these ordinary men displayed greater influence than the best and brightest of their generation?

The answer is, they were *holy men of God*. Their lives were transformed by Jesus. They were trusting and obeying Him and living in the power of the Spirit.

The rulers asked Peter and John, "By what power or by what name have you done this?" (Acts 4:7). Peter answered, "By the name of Jesus Christ of Nazareth. . . . For there is no other name under heaven given among men by which we must be saved" (vv. 10–12).

Peter announced that the name of Jesus was the source of salvation and the source of power for daily living. Peter's holiness was not a one-time fix, but rather a daily relationship with Jesus.

What is holiness? Holiness is Christlikeness. Continual fellowship with Jesus provides constant power to live and serve. Holiness becomes, as Bible commentator W. T. Purkiser observed, a "throbbing, pulsating connection with the divine dynamo."

Twice in Acts 4 we're told that Peter and John followed God's holy Servant. The source of their holiness was "Jesus," and everything they did was done in His name. They *healed* in Jesus' name; they *taught* in Jesus' name; they *worked* in Jesus' name (3:1–11; 4:10, 18–20, 30). Jesus was their source.

Whose name and power will we draw on this week? It seems that there are two ruts to avoid. The first is blind Christianity; the second, dumb Christianity.

By blind Christianity, I mean those who claim to be Jesus' disciples but have no deeds to prove it. No one can see their faith lived out. This Christianity is mostly talk and no action.

Dumb Christianity, conversely, is seen in those who abound in good deeds but never act in a definite name. For all we know, they might be secular humanists or hardworking cultists. Who will ever know the source of your life and service if you do not speak in Jesus' name?

Peter and John avoided both extremes. Their witness was clear, and they served in the unmistakable name of Jesus. He was the foundation of their holiness.

Acts 4 suggests several marks of a holy life.

It can't be explained. It has often been said that if you can explain it, God didn't do it. The ministry of Jesus and the disciples defied human explanation (John 7:15; Acts 4:13). Left to itself, the Christian church should have died centuries ago. Only the power of God accounts for the church's preservation.

It can't be denied. The opposition lamented, "What shall we do to these men? For, indeed, that a notable miracle has been done through them is evident to all who dwell in Jerusalem, and we cannot deny it" (Acts 4:16). Do we display undeniable supernatural power?

It can't be intimidated. A holy life revolutionizes its surroundings. Approximately five thousand men heard and believed the gospel (v. 4). In spite of threats, Peter and John refused to be silent.

It can't stop praying. Peter and John prayed, and "the place where they were assembled together was shaken; and they were all filled with the Holy Spirit, and they spoke the word of God with boldness" (v. 31).

Holiness is primarily the quality of life that comes from *trusting and obeying* Jesus. It's God's character rubbing off on our character. This holiness becomes ours as we allow the Holy Spirit to mold our lives. To miss the call to a holy life is, in essence, to miss the Christian life.

1 6

Small Things

"The bigger, the better."

"Supersize it!"

"I can't wait to make it big and start living large."

Our world has been taught to evaluate success in terms of size—bigger cars, bigger houses, bigger trust funds, and so forth. However, bigger is not necessarily better—or even desirable. When people are mesmerized by size, they can become impersonal, insensitive, and even incapable of responding to others' needs with compassion.

Life, in reality, is enhanced by many small things: a tiny seed, a little baby, a single word, a momentary smile, a small courtesy, or an apparent trifle. It's humbling to remember that man was created from "the dust of the ground" (Genesis 2:7)—not from gold or diamonds, but dust. Even the word *humanity* comes from the Latin *humus,* meaning "decayed vegetable matter."

When God called Moses to lead the Israelites out of bondage, He didn't speak through a giant oak or a towering cedar, but through a small desert bush. To confirm His call, God transformed the staff of Moses into "the rod of God."

The staff was just an ordinary stick, probably about six feet long. Possibly Moses had carried this staff for forty years as he tended his desert flock. It's encouraging to remember that God enjoys using small things. With his shepherd's staff, Moses went on to confront the powers of Egypt. The plagues fell upon all Egypt as Moses lifted his rod (Exodus 7–12). On a later occasion, God used the rod of Moses to divide the Red Sea as the children of Israel made their escape (14:16). Still later, God used the rod of Moses to supply water for the Israelites as they journeyed through the wilderness (17:5–6). The rod in itself was nothing, yet under God's might it became an instrument of power.

Size and spiritual power are not synonymous. In fact, the Scriptures often indicate the opposite. When God told His people to build a sanctuary, it was to be different from the pagan temples. The tabernacle for the eternal God was to include boards and badgers' skins (25:5).

We again see God's use of "small things" in Israel's defeat of the Canaanite general Sisera, as recorded in Judges 4. Sisera fled by foot all the way to the tent of Jael, the wife of Heber. Exhausted, he asked for water. Instead, she gave him milk, and soon he fell into a deep sleep. As he slept, Jael "took a tent peg and took a hammer in her hand, and went softly to him and drove the peg into his temple, and it went down into the ground. . . . So he died" (Judges 4:21). Jael killed him, not with a shimmering arrow, a sleek spear, or a mighty sword, but a tent peg.

Often God used small things: dust, a bush, a rod, boards and badgers' skins, a jawbone, five smooth stones and a sling, or a boy's lunch of five loaves and two small fish. The principle is spelled out by Paul: "God has chosen the weak things of the world to put to shame the things which are mighty; and the base things of the world and the things which are despised God has chosen" (1 Corinthians 1:27–28).

Why? "That no flesh should glory in His presence" (v. 29).

God uses small things so that everyone will know that the credit belongs to God alone.

Remember, when Jesus came to earth, He was not born in Rome or Athens or even Jerusalem, but in Bethlehem, "little among the thousands of Judah" (Micah 5:2). Jesus was not only born in Bethlehem's manger, but He was raised in lowly Nazareth. His followers, for the most part, were not the elite, but hardworking common people.

Paul reminds us, "We have this treasure in earthen vessels, that the excellence of the power may be of God and not of us" (2 Corinthians 4:7).

So whoever you are and whatever you have, bring it to Jesus. It may seem like a small thing to you, but there's no limit to what He might do with it.

1 7

Love Endures

While running the semi-finals of the 400-meter race in the 1992 Olympics, Derek Redmond pulled a muscle two-thirds of the way through the race. Though the cheering crowd would have understood if he had dropped out, he limped the rest of the way until he crossed the finish line. He refused to quit!

God's love is like that! Divine love is both tender and tough. We are taught to be "tenderhearted, forgiving one another, just as God in Christ also forgave you" (Ephesians 4:32). Without doubt, God's love is tenderhearted, but divine love also knows how to *endure* (1 Corinthians 13:7). The word *endure* in the original language means "to remain under . . . to persevere . . . not to quit."

An esteemed business friend, Maxey Jarmen, told me of a life-changing decision he made while still in his early twenties. Though by nature a shy person, he was asked to teach the large men's class at his local Nashville church. His father strongly encouraged him to accept the challenge and give it all he had—to become the best teacher possible. Maxey placed himself under the authority of God and the authority of his local church.

He told me that two significant things happened as a result of his decision. First, he became a serious and able student of Scripture. Second, he learned how to effectively communicate with others. Maxey Jarmen continued to teach that class for over forty years and, during that time, developed an apparel company that numbered some 75,000 employees. His company became the largest apparel company in the world. "It all began," said Maxey, "when I placed my life under the authority of God and under the authority of my local church."

Too often the followers of Jesus choose not to be under authority. Some walk out of earthly obligations, wanting no authority but their own. Repeatedly, we're taught in the Scriptures to be "submissive to one another" (1 Peter 5:5; see also Hebrews 13:17).

While Jesus was in the Garden of Gethsemane, He placed Himself under His Father's authority. He prayed, "Father, if it is Your will, remove this cup from Me; nevertheless not My will, but Yours, be done" (Luke 22:42).

His tender love also demonstrated toughness during His crucifixion. After He had suffered indescribably, "They filled a sponge with vinegar, and put it upon hyssop, and put it to his mouth. When Jesus therefore had received the vinegar, he said, It is finished" (John 19:29–30 KJV).

As we learn to submit to the authority of God, we too can cultivate a love that doesn't quit. Let us finish the job God has given us, for God's love "endures all things" (1 Corinthians 13:7).

1 8

Pressure Produces

Out of the presses of pain
Comes the soul's best wine.
The eyes that have shed no rain,
Can shed but little shine.

(A.B. Simpson)

Sometimes positive change comes only as a result of pressure. It's the crushed flower that gives perfume. It's the squeezed fruit that yields the juice. Pressure pounds and pulverizes rock into rich soil and creates beautiful diamonds from rougher forms of carbon.

An ordinary bar of steel costs only a few dollars. If it is hammered into horseshoes, its price doubles. Made into needles, its value escalates a hundred times. Fashioned into springs for fine watches, its worth becomes incalculable.

Could it be that God allows us to be heated and hammered in order to hone our gifts and increase our worth? I believe so. These tests of life are not given to *destroy* us, but to *demonstrate* God's ability in and through us. Several things should be remembered about life's pressures:

1. *Everyone has pressures.* People with sunny dispositions appear immune to pressures. However, no one is exempt.

2. *Pressures are temporary.* They may appear to be permanent, but for the most part they are temporary. They will pass.

3. *Pressures are opportunities for our development and must not be wasted.* Bumps are the things we climb on!

Jesus promised, "In the world you will have tribulation; but be of good cheer, I have overcome the world" (John 16:33).

What do pressures produce? James tells us that pressure "produces *endurance*" (James 1:3 NASB, italics added). God permits tests in our lives to make us *stronger* and to solidify our faith. Pressure plus faith in God produces consistency and a sterling character.

The threshing sledge sometimes used in Bible times to beat the grain and divide the chaff from the wheat was called a *tribulum* in Latin, from *tribulāre,* "to press." The English word *tribulation* comes from this word. Trials separate the chaff from the wheat in our lives; they help to reduce selfishness and encourage caring.

C. B. Williams translates James 1:4: "Let your endurance come to its perfect product, so that you may be fully developed and perfectly equipped." Pressure produces completeness. I think James was saying, "Don't try to wiggle out of your trials."

A story is told of a boy with two cocoons. He watched a beautiful butterfly emerge from the first cocoon and couldn't wait to see what would come from the second one. He took a pen knife and cut a small opening, hoping to assist the butterfly. When the butterfly emerged, it was incapacitated. The struggle to exit the cocoon was necessary to help it fully develop its wings. Without the struggle, it didn't have the strength to fly.

Our times of pressure are often blessings, even when they seem like useless struggles. May we accept them, not with resentment, but with full trust in a wise and loving God. Pressure produces!

1 9

God's Remedy for Worry

Many tombstones contain epitaphs that are clever, touching, and creative. However, a more *truthful* remembrance in many cases would probably be "Died of worry."

Psalm 37 offers a prescription to eliminate the harmful symptoms of worry. David is surrounded by his enemies and the situation appears bleak. Yet he was able to say, "Do not fret because of evildoers, nor be envious of the workers of iniquity" (v. 1).

Webster defines the word *fret* as "to suffer emotional strain, or to eat or gnaw into, or to become uneasy, vexed, or worried." David recommends, "Don't get into perilous heat over things." In today's language, "Don't lose your cool," "Hang loose," "Keep calm," "Don't sweat it."

Worry reveals a basic distrust in God. According to Psalm 73, the evildoers were prospering. David sensed that some of the people had begun to look at the success of the ungodly and were dismayed. Of course, there are times when the unbelieving appear to prosper in this world: "They increase in riches" (v. 12). At first, David didn't understand this. It caused him worry. Then he "went into the sanctuary of God" and "understood their end" (v. 17).

We need to remember that the prosperity of the unbelieving is for time—not eternity. "They shall soon be cut down like the grass, and wither as the green herb" (Psalm 37:2). Their success is brief.

"Don't fret," David said, because fretting heats the bearing but doesn't generate power. A hot axle hinders progress. Psalm 37 suggests a fivefold cure for care.

1. *Trust in the Lord* (v. 3). The word translated "trust" throughout the Old Testament means "without care," or literally, "careless." To be careless doesn't mean flippant, but rather a freedom from care. It's the confidence of a little child at play, knowing that his parents are present and he is safe. It's a positive trust and cooperation with the will of God. It is 1 Peter 5:7, "Casting all your anxiety on Him, because He cares for you" (NASB).

2. *Trust in the Lord, and do good* (v. 3). Doing good is a *solid cure for worry*. Doing good is a wholesome activity. Work is healthy. Work rarely kills people—worry does.

If you are smothered by care, I encourage you to become genuinely interested in others. Do something good for someone today.

3. *Delight yourself . . . in the Lord* (v. 4). Literally, David was saying, "Seek for the delicacies that are to be found in knowing God." Learn of His wisdom, His power, His patience, and His compassion.

Verse 4 promises, "And He shall give you the desires of your heart."

4. *Commit your way to the Lord* (v. 5). Put God in charge of your life. Let Him have complete control. Cast all your trouble and opportunities on Him, and He will bring you peace.

5. *Rest in the Lord* (v. 7). If we take the first four steps prescribed by David, we can enjoy a *special rest* that only God can provide.

We can't avoid being beset by worry from time to time. The difference between overcoming worry and being defeated by it is remembering that God has a remedy—and then following His prescription.

2 0

Does Character Count?

The four classic character traits of the ancient world were wisdom, courage, temperance, and justice. Christianity added to these traits faith, hope, and love. For centuries, these characteristics served as the basis of moral virtues.

Our Declaration of Independence from England calls attention to the deficient character of King George III, noting his "long train of abuses." It continues to say, "A Prince, whose character is marked by every act which may be defined a Tyrant, is unfit to be the ruler of a free people."

George Washington, America's first president, was praised for his sterling character. Some historians suggest that it was his good character that gave credibility to the new constitution.

P. B. Fitzwater, a former professor at the Moody Bible Institute, defined character as "the sum and total of a person's choices." Our daily choices slowly and surely shape our character.

Writer Oscar Wilde once confessed:

> I let myself be lured into long spells of senseless and sensual ease. . . . Tired of being on the heights, I deliberately went to the depths in search of a new sensation. . . . I grew careless of the lives of others. *I forgot that every little action of the common day makes or unmakes character,* and that therefore what one has done in the secret chamber, one has some day to cry aloud from the house-top.

God is more concerned with character than external appearances, according to 1 Samuel 16:7. Proverbs instructs, "Keep your heart with all diligence, for out of it spring the issues of life" (Proverbs 4:23).

Jesus not only exemplified sterling character, but specializes in remaking those who commit their lives to Him (2 Corinthians 5:17).

While visiting the cemetery at Princeton University I discovered the gravestone of Aaron Burr. The inscription read, "Colonel in the Continental Army, Vice President of the United States." Near his grave are those of his godly father, the Reverend Aaron Burr, second president of Princeton; and his famous grandfather, Jonathan Edwards, theologian and evangelist.

Aaron Burr had all that heredity and Christianity could give a person, but, unfortunately, he also had a flawed character.

Burr so distinguished himself in the early years of the Revolutionary War that he was placed on General George Washington's staff. But he was soon transferred because of differences with his superior.

After the war, his legal brilliance was recognized. He was elected to the New York State Assembly and later appointed attorney general. At the age of thirty-five he was elected to the United States Senate, and in 1800 was nominated as vice president on the Jefferson ticket.

Through an odd blunder in the electoral process, Burr received as many electoral votes as Thomas Jefferson, which threw the final decision into the House of Representatives.

Then began the historic feud between Burr and Alexander Hamilton. Hamilton's determined opposition to Burr finally led to Jefferson's election. But rumors said that Burr connived to wrest the presidency from his chief, so that Jefferson never trusted him. When Burr tried to retrieve his political fortunes, Hamilton again threw his influence against him as a "dangerous" man. Embittered, Burr challenged Hamilton to the famous duel.

The shot that killed Hamilton indirectly killed Burr. He became an outcast from his country's social and political life. He fled to Europe, where for years he wandered from country to country. Eventually, Burr returned to New York in disguise. He lived in obscurity for twenty-two years until his death and then was carried to Princeton and buried near his godly father and grandfather.

The sad story of Aaron Burr reminds us that character does count. Ultimately, success depends not on the dreams we dream, but on the *choices* we make!

21

My Boyhood Pastor

Since it began in 1925, the Hawthorne Gospel Church has hosted guests such as Harry Ironside, Donald Grey Barnhouse, Martin Lloyd Jones, Robert G. Lee, A. W. Tozer, and Billy Graham. For the first sixty-two years, the church had the same pastor, a man who never became well known. When asked why he stayed so long at the same place, Herrmann George Braunlin modestly answered, "No one ever asked me to leave."

My boyhood pastor was a role model for me and many others. During a lifetime of ministry, I have regularly asked myself, *How would Pastor Braunlin handle this situation?*

Even though he never attended college or seminary, he was a capable teacher, talented administrator, and brilliant visionary. Seldom have I seen a more innovative church than the Hawthorne Gospel Church. Forty years ago, Pastor Braunlin advised the congregation to relocate to choice acreage along a strategic highway leading directly to New York City. Few agreed with his vision for relocation at first, yet today all enthusiastically agree that it was a move of genius.

Other of his programs included a "Bible House," which retails Christian literature to a major metropolitan area; a quality evening school that has greatly influenced the area for more than fifty years; a lending library used by churches of every denomination; a day-care center; and a secondary school—all in addition to conventional church outreaches. During his lifetime, he received significant honors. But he was a genuinely humble man who did not mention his awards to his congregation.

Pastor Braunlin was a man of the Bible and of prayer. He faithfully taught the Bible, verse by verse, Genesis 1:1 to Revelation 22:21. And regardless of the occasion, earnest prayer was the norm. To him, praying was as necessary as breathing.

All of us need at least three people in our lives: a Paul, a Barnabas, and a Timothy. A Barnabas is an equal partner in our service, and a Timothy is a younger person in the faith who is eager to learn and grow. But Pastor Braunlin was a Paul to me—a beloved friend and counselor.

On October 5, 1995, Herrmann G. Braunlin was promoted into the presence of God. Over one thousand friends attended his memorial service to express affection for him and to give thanks to God for a loving, hardworking pastor.

Thankfully, each of us has an Eternal Pastor, who is always available and has promised to *never* leave us (Hebrews 13:5). He remains the author—and *finisher*—of our faith.

2 2

Coping with Conflicts

A few years ago, a Norwegian statistician computerized every war that had ever been fought. His study indicated that during 5,560 years of recorded history there have been 14,531 wars, averaging more than 2.6 wars each year. In our 185 generations, only 10 of those generations have witnessed unbroken peace. Throughout history, conflicts have been the rule and peace the exception. Why?

Abraham Lincoln was once walking with his two sons, both of whom were fighting. "What's the matter with your boys?" a passerby asked. "Exactly what is wrong with the whole world," Lincoln said. "I have three walnuts, and each boy wants two."

Family conflicts, gang fights, and global wars all originate from the same selfish desires. James asked, "Where do wars and fights come from among you? Do they not come from your desires for pleasure that war in your members?" (James 4:1).

The word *desire* used here speaks of unsatisfied evil desires. In his letter to young Timothy, Paul told of being deserted by his friend Demas because he "loved this present world" (2 Timothy 4:10). The tug of earthly possessions and pleasures spoiled Demas's partnership with Paul.

At the outset of World War II, Hitler defended his aggression by declaring that Germany needed more living space. James reminded his readers that the craving for more is the root of all conflict.

I will never forget the speech by General Douglas MacArthur when Japan surrendered to the United States at the close of the conflict. Referring to the continuing threat of war, MacArthur said: "Military alliance, balances of power, the League of Nations—all in turn have failed. We have had our last chance. If we do not devise some greater and more equitable system, Armageddon will be at our door. The problem, basically, is theological. . . . It must be of the spirit if we are to save the flesh."

The problem of conflict is spiritual. It really doesn't make much difference where strife is found. The origin of a family squabble or the cause of a world conflict can both be traced to human selfishness.

R. V. G. Tasker said in *The General Epistle of James:*

Human nature is indeed in the grip of an overwhelming army of occupation. Its natural aim, it can truthfully be said, is pleasure; and when we consider the amount of time, energy, money, interest and enthusiasm that men and women give to the satisfaction of this aim, we can appreciate the accuracy of James' diagnosis; and Christians can use it as a reliable yardstick by which to measure the sincerity of their religion. Is God or pleasure the dominant concern of their life?

Man's basic need is for a spiritual birth. A new nature is required, one that God alone can impart. Only then will our desires be what they ought to be.

Allow me to suggest a few ways we might cope with conflicts in our lives.

First, *seek the mind of Christ.* Paul wrote concerning two individuals in the church at Philippi: "I implore Euodia and I implore Syntyche to be of the same mind in the Lord" (Philippians 4:2). We can be of one mind as we seek and submit to the mind of Christ. Thank God, these selfish desires of ours can be put right.

How do we deal with sources of strife? As Paul wrote to the Philippians, "It is God who works in you both to will and to do for His good pleasure" (2:13). It's God alone who can work in us. Only He can give us the right desires and help us do His will.

Second, *rely upon the indwelling Holy Spirit.* We, in ourselves, cannot expect to overcome evil desires. But we can draw upon the power of the One who indwells us. Paul said, "Reckon yourselves to be dead indeed to sin, but alive to God in Christ Jesus" (Romans 6:11).

Instead of being a slave to sin, bound by lusts, I am in Christ Jesus alive and alert to His desires. Strife is manageable when I commit myself to the Lord.

The key to solving conflict is found in submitting to God's will. When we do this, our desires become His desires and His power becomes our power.

Third, *ask God for things with right motives.* James wrote, "You ask and do not receive, because you ask amiss, that you may spend it on your pleasures" (James 4:3).

The glory and honor of God is our supreme purpose for existing.

Finally, remember that in spite of the promise of conflicts and even war itself, Jesus said, "My peace I give to you" (John 14:27). When we live with this focus, we find grace and strength . . . to cope with every conflict.

That Which
I Should Have Done,
I Did Not Do

Ivan Le Lorraine Albright's ten-year masterpiece hangs in the Art Institute of Chicago. The painting is of an eight-foot-high door shaped like the lid of a casket.

The door is scarred and marred by the bruising experiences of life. A somber mood is created by the use of black and deep blue grays and smudges of red.

A crepe of dead roses and lily of the valleys hangs on the door. A wrinkled yet tender hand rests with seeming regret upon the molding of the door that can no longer be opened.

The painting's doorstep is a tombstone rubbed clean of the epitaph, suggesting that neglected opportunities become lost opportunities. Albright titled this painting, "That Which I Should Have Done, I Did Not Do."

There is a strong tendency in life to think of the sins of omission as less deadly than the sins of commission. We have the idea that it's more serious to do what we shouldn't do than to fail to do what we should. But neglected opportunities become lost opportunities.

Jesus illustrated this in His parable of the ten virgins (Matthew 25:1–13). The five wise virgins were fully prepared for the arrival of the bridegroom. Their lamps were filled with oil and burning brightly. The five foolish virgins delayed and slept until they were awakened by the call of the advancing bridegroom. In their confusion, they rushed to buy oil for their lamps and missed the wedding celebration. The five foolish virgins were not anti-bridegroom nor anti-God. They were simply preoccupied and unprepared. The Scripture adds these words: "And the door was shut" (v. 10), followed by a warning: "Watch therefore, for you know neither the day nor the hour in which the Son of Man is coming" (v. 13).

Unused talents evaporate! Unclaimed opportunities vanish! Unentered doors close!

A similar picture appears in the account of Noah and the divine call to enter the ark. Following God's gracious invitation, "Come into the ark, you and all your household" (Genesis 7:1), the Scripture reads, "And the Lord shut him in" (v. 16). Again, this story implies that neglected opportunities are lost opportunities, that no answer is an answer, that indecision is a decision, that open doors shut.

Scripture reminds us, "To him who knows to do good and does not do it, to him it is sin" (James 4:17). Simply put, the sins of omission are as fatal as the sins of commission.

Sunday, October 8, 1871, was the night of the great Chicago fire. Evangelist D. L. Moody spoke to a capacity crowd at Farwell Hall on the subject, "What then should I do with Jesus, who is called the Christ?"

His soloist, Ira D. Sankey, sang:

Today the Savior calls,
For refuge fly!
The storm of Justice falls,
And death is nigh!

In spite of Sankey's imploring song, Moody told his audience, "Take this text home with you and turn it over in your minds, and next Sabbath . . . decide what to do with Jesus of Nazareth."[1]

Moody later confessed that this was the worst mistake he had ever made. He never saw that congregation again. The great fire consumed 3.5 square miles, destroying 1,800 buildings and leaving 90,000 people homeless and 300 dead. "I have never dared to give an audience a week to think over their salvation since."[2] Moody failed to do what he should have done and never forgot it.

Luke 19 tells of a person who was given a large sum of money but did nothing to use it or to increase it. Instead, he wrapped the money in a handkerchief, supposedly for safekeeping, and buried it. Even though this individual was innocent of any gross act of commission, Jesus condemned him because he failed to use the opportunity that was his. In other words, that which he should have done, he didn't do.

Ivan Albright's painting reminds me of another door—one mentioned in Revelation 3:20. Jesus says, "I stand at the door and knock. If anyone hears My voice and opens the door, I will come in to him and dine with him, and he with Me." Let us not omit responding to this divine knock. Behind the door, lie untold opportunities.

NOTES

1. William R. Moody, *The Life of Dwight L. Moody* (Chicago: Revell, 1900), 144.

2. Ibid., 145.

2 4

Be Kind

Everyone you meet is carrying a burden. Though not everyone shows it, our world is starving for kindness. The word *kind* comes from *kin,* or *kindred,* and carries in its meaning the idea of love for those who are our own flesh and blood. Goethe expanded the definition when he said, "Kindness is the golden chain by which society is bound together."

Our human tendency is to be hasty, quick tempered, and unkind. We may even try to separate love from kindness. I recall being misunderstood and criticized by a friend whom I expected would know better. I desperately wanted to retaliate, but with bulldog determination I clenched my fist, bit my lip, and managed to keep my mouth closed. I kept silent, but surely I was not genuinely kind, gracious, or loving.

Kindness and love are inseparable and should be the marks of every believer. We need to develop the patient willingness to endure criticism and misunderstanding. Usually such patience is exhausted just when it is needed most. G. K. Chesterton observed: "There is no such thing as being a gentleman at important moments; it is at unimportant moments that a man is a gentleman. . . . If once his mind is possessed in any strong degree with the knowledge that he is a gentleman, he will soon cease to be one."

Kindness was important to the apostle Paul. When he described the qualities of love in 1 Corinthians 13:4, he included the statement, "Love suffers long and is kind." He told the Ephesians, "Be kind to one another, tenderhearted, forgiving one another, just as God in Christ also forgave you" (Ephesians 4:32).

Jesus Christ was kind to others and asked His followers to do the same: "But love your enemies, do good, and lend, hoping for nothing in return; and your reward will be great, and you will be sons of the Highest. For He is kind to the unthankful and evil" (Luke 6:35).

Our Savior was kind even though He was often misunderstood. For thirty-three years He went about ministering to the sick, feeding the hungry, comforting the bereaved, and always helping others. He was patiently kind to His disciples, to the sick who crowded in on Him, to Pilate, and to the crucified thief. Even in His dying hours after the nails had done their ugly work, He called out, "Father, forgive them, for they do not know what they do" (Luke 23:34). His degree of kindness is beyond human understanding yet is the very attitude of love that God would live through us.

God showed His kindness by forgiving us. Don't we have an obligation to extend that same kindness . . . to others?

2 5

God's Favorite Word

Many people have words or phrases they tend to use over and over again. Although no one fully knows the mind of God, I have a feeling that He too has some special words. One word in particular seems to echo throughout the Bible. It was used to transform Peter from a rugged fisherman into a devoted follower of Jesus. It was spoken by Jesus to the little children who flocked around Him. I believe God's favorite word . . . is the word *Come!*

Come is the great word of the gospel. *Go* was the significant word of the Law, pointing out the gulf between God and man. But the gospel bridges that gulf, reconciling us to God and providing a way to escape judgment for our sins. God's ongoing invitation is, "Come to Me" (Matthew 11:28).

David Brainerd was a great missionary statesman, but at seventeen he was confused about God's salvation. He wrote, "I thought I would gladly come to Jesus, but I had no directions as to getting through." Yet as he prayed, Brainerd thought, *When a mother tells her child to come to her, she does not tell him how to come. He may come with a run, a jump, a skip, or a leap. He may come praying, shouting, singing, or even crying. It doesn't matter how he comes, so long as he comes.*

The same thing is true regarding God's salvation. It does not matter how we come to Christ. The important thing is that we do come to Him. We are to come just as we are.

The hands of Jesus often were extended to lift the fallen, bless the little children, and heal the sick. His hands were wide open on the cross when He was crucified. Those very hands stretch out to all, saying, "Come with your fears, your frustrations, and your sins." Someone has made an acrostic of the word *come*. *C* is for children, *O* is for old, *M* is for the middle-aged, *E* is for everybody. The fact is that God wants everyone to come to Him.

The last verses in the Bible extend God's all-inclusive invitation as a fitting climax to the Bible. Revelation 22:17 says: "And the Spirit and the bride say, 'Come!' And let him who hears say, 'Come!' And let him who thirsts come. And whoever desires, let him take the water of life freely."

God the Father, God the Son, and God the Holy Spirit say, "Come." The church, the bride of Christ, says, "Come." The best possible response to God's favorite word . . . is to "come."

2 6

The Great Depression

My father arrived in the United States from Glasgow, Scotland, in 1923. My parents lived in a rented house in Haledon, New Jersey, and I was born there in October of 1924. Dad was a bricklayer and work was plentiful, so the following May, he bought a six-room dream home at a cost of $4,900, and it remained the family home for over fifty years.

Dad's letters to Scotland sparkled with optimism as he raved about the availability of food and work—until the stock market crashed on October 24, 1929! As the country moved into the Great Depression, Dad could no longer find work in his trade. In desperation, he took a job as a night watchman at a silk mill, working from midnight until eight o'clock in the morning, for $28 a week.

I would not choose to relive the Depression days, yet they taught my family many life-building lessons. First, we learned *the impor-*

tance of each member of the family as we struggled to meet the monthly mortgage payment. Mother took in washing and ironing. Brother Bill and I sold magazines door-to-door. The three boys helped deliver milk. We all made hat bands for a nearby hat factory, made and sold paper flowers, and did what we could to conserve heat and electricity.

At one point, a "For Sale" sign was posted on our home. As potential buyers came, we children earnestly prayed that the prospective buyer wouldn't like the house and did a few things . . . to our shame . . . to make the house appear less attractive. At the depth of the crisis, family friends extended a loan to allow us to buy our home.

The Depression days also taught us *thrift and old-fashioned frugality* (though as a Scottish family, we were already teased about how thrifty we were). When we used tea bags, we did so again and again. The phone was an absolute luxury, used only for emergencies. One electric light was allowed on per room. Usually, we all studied and worked in a single room. To this day, dimly lit restaurants depress me.

We also learned the value of money and the importance of avoiding credit. Mother used to say, "If your *outgo* is greater than your *income,* then your *upkeep* is headed for a *downfall.*" We were often reminded of Paul's words, "Owe no one anything" (Romans 13:8).

Finally, the Great Depression was a major factor *in strengthening our faith.* I have since discovered that a few years of poverty can do more for spiritual maturity than ten years of prosperity.

It was a difficult time, but I can look back with much gratitude for the lessons learned during the Great Depression!

God Cares
About Your Tears

Centuries ago, Solomon observed, "To everything there is a season, a time for every purpose under heaven: . . . A time to weep, and a time to laugh; a time to mourn, and a time to dance" (Ecclesiastes 3:1–4).

David, Solomon's father, also talked about *tears.* "You number my wanderings; put my tears into Your bottle; are they not in Your book?" (Psalm 56:8).

Some people in Bible times apparently collected their tears in a bottle made of animal skins. David reminds each of us that God is not only aware of our tears, but *records* and even *preserves* them.

The gospel of Luke speaks of a woman who was grateful to Jesus. "[She] stood at His feet behind Him weeping; and she began to wash His feet with her tears, and wiped them with the hair of her head;

and she kissed His feet and anointed them with the fragrant oil" (Luke 7:38)

The tear bottle was symbolic of all the heart-wrenching experiences of life. Eloquently, it spoke of the compassionate interest and tender care God has for each of us. God cares about our sorrows and records our tears.

Jesus shed tears on at least two occasions: once at the grave of His beloved friend, Lazarus (John 11:35), and again as He looked across His beloved city, Jerusalem: "He saw the city and wept over it" (Luke 19:41).

Often the Bible speaks about *tears of repentance.* After Peter denied Jesus, he remembered Christ's prediction and "went out and *wept bitterly*" (Matthew 26:75, italics added). Though tears can be traumatic, there must be genuine repentance before they are acceptable to God.

The Scriptures also speak about the *tears of service.* The apostle Paul gave us a glimpse of his ministry to the Ephesians. "I [served] the Lord with all humility, with many tears," he said (Acts 20:19).

Writing to the Christians in Rome, Paul shared his concern for his people, Israel. "For I could wish that I myself were accursed from Christ for my brethren, my kinsmen according to the flesh" (Romans 9:3). To the Corinthian congregation, Paul penned, "For out of much affliction and anguish of heart I wrote to you, with many tears" (2 Corinthians 2:4).

Expressing deep love for his spiritual son, Timothy, Paul wrote, "[I am] greatly desiring to see you, being mindful of your tears, that I may be filled with joy" (2 Timothy 1:4).

I heard of a Salvation Army worker who failed in his efforts to share the Good News. In desperation, he wrote to General Booth and said, "I've tried everything. What shall I try now?"

General Booth telegraphed two words: "Try tears."

Why is God interested in our tears? Because He deeply cares for us and will reward us for our tears someday.

Jeremiah's tear bottle must have been overflowing. He wrote, "Oh, that my head were waters, and my eyes a fountain of tears, that I might weep day and night for the slain of the daughter of my people!" (Jeremiah 9:1).

The tear bottle probably had markings along the side to record the anguish of life's journey. On one occasion, David's situation must have been desperate. He wrote, "I am weary with my groaning; all night I make my bed swim; I drench my couch with my tears" (Psalm 6:6). Have you ever felt like that?

Someday each of us will be able to do what the woman of Luke 7 did: empty our tears at the feet of Jesus. From the Garden of Eden until now, many tears have been shed. But there is coming a great day when there will be . . . no more tears!

The apostle John gives us a picture of the final day when "God will wipe away every tear from their eyes; there shall be no more death, nor sorrow, nor crying; and there shall be no more pain" (Revelation 21:4).

God really cares about your tears. But as we weep over the sad situations of life, let us look forward to a day when our tears will be a thing of the past.

2 8

Blessed
Are the Balanced

Occasionally on our daily walks, my wife, Hilda, teasingly reminds me to stop my groaning. To which I reply, "Why should I? It's biblical."

I am convinced that it's natural to be negative. Ever since the failure of Adam and Eve, all of creation has been "groaning." Whether it's the wailing wind, the pounding surf, a bleating sheep, a barking dog, or even a singing bird, they all speak in a minor key to remind us of the sin in our world (Genesis 3:14–19).

Paul writes about this groaning, "We know that the whole creation groans and labors with birth pangs together until now. And not only they, but we also who have the firstfruits of the Spirit, even we ourselves groan within ourselves, eagerly waiting for the adoption, the redemption of our body" (Romans 8:22–23). Based on that passage in particular, I conclude that it is natural to be negative!

However, along with the truth of human failure, there is the mind-stretching truth of divine deliverance. Paul eloquently wrote: "If by one man's offense [Adam] death reigned . . . *much more* those who receive abundance of grace and of the gift of righteousness *will reign* in life through the One, Jesus Christ" (Romans 5:17, italics added).

The gospel has the power to move us from pessimism to optimism, from despair to triumph. Of course, both pessimism and optimism can be carried to extremes. Constant pessimism can be depressing, whereas extreme optimism can be unrealistic. It's been said that a pessimist is someone who is seasick for the whole journey of life and that when two pessimists meet, they don't shake hands, they just shake heads.

On the other hand, the perpetual optimist is unrealistic. A friend of mine defines an optimist as a person with "misty optics." In my unsanctified moments, I have occasionally mimicked an acquaintance whose life is always and everywhere absolutely perfect! Some years ago, I coined an uncanonical beatitude: "Blessed are the balanced."

Balance is the mingling of optimism and pessimism. It is not a Jekyll and Hyde, but a David and Jonathan, a Paul and Timothy, working in unison, inspiring and encouraging each other.

Imbalance can be hurtful. In doctrine, it can result in heresy. Extreme self-examination can be unhealthy, whereas neglect of introspection can result in carelessness and indifference. Balance is the key to a healthy life, both physically and spiritually. I find great inspiration from the words of the apostle Paul in Philippians 4:12–13: "I know how to be abased, and I know how to abound. Everywhere and in all things I have learned both to be full and to be hungry, both to abound and to suffer need. I can do all things through Christ who strengthens me."

Sometimes God loads our arms with blessings and our backs with burdens. As we learn to deal with both situations, He teaches us to remain balanced!

2 9

Ultimate Success

A business friend of D. L. Moody's owned a meat-packing company. When people asked his occupation, he would answer, "I serve Jesus, but pack pork to pay expenses." Some of the greatest Christians I know have other occupations to pay expenses. They've been boatbuilders, bankers, truckers, farmers, sales representatives, teachers—the list goes on. But serving Christ and His church is a primary call.

Each of us needs at least three ingredients for ultimate success: a self fit to live with, a faith fit to live by, and a work fit to live for. Do these three things apply to you?

First, do you have *a self* fit to live with, or are you living with a self that makes each day a drag? The issue here is personal faith in Christ. If you need a self fit to live with, the answer is found in Him. Jesus majors in changing people.

Second, do you have *a faith* fit to live by? If you're a Christian, you should be building a faith to live by. Many people begin the Christian life only to fall by the wayside. My friend, you need to keep growing! Read that Bible and live it—each day. Pray. Tell others about your faith. Find a strong church and make it yours. Then you will enjoy an exciting, growing, vital faith—a faith fit to live by.

The third requirement needs to be emphasized. You need *a work* fit to live for. Do you have an inner calling that drives you? Eating, sleeping, and making payments on a house aren't enough. Enjoying your work, getting ahead, and building a reputation will not satisfy. You hitch your wagon to a star only when you discover *a work worth all you can give it.*

Paul's letter to the Philippians was written from inside a Roman jail, but it overflows with optimism because he had *a work fit to live for.*

Listen to Paul's words: "I want you to know, brethren, that the things which happened to me have actually turned out for the furtherance of the gospel" (Philippians 1:12). A little later, Paul expressed his ultimate goal: "That in nothing I shall be ashamed, but that with all boldness, as always, so now also Christ will be magnified in my body, whether by life or by death" (v. 20)!

Are you living at this level? You can. Jesus challenged individuals with two simple, life-changing words: "Follow Me." Matthew, Andrew, Peter, James, John, and others like them, left all, rose up, and followed. Following Jesus appears to be a simple act, and yet contained in these words is the ultimate secret of success.

What does it mean to follow Jesus? Does Jesus still ask men and women to follow Him today? Yes, He does! To follow Jesus means *to make Him first in your life.* It means putting aside your personal program to get involved in His eternal program.

That's exactly what the disciples did. Andrew, Peter, James, and John were in the fishing business, but when Jesus called them, they left it all behind. Matthew probably worked for years to gain his position as a tax collector, but when Jesus came along, he made a choice. He left his table and title. The point is not that they changed occupations. No, they switched from serving themselves to serving Jesus. They took up *serving in a greater cause.*

Have you done that? If your life seems hardly worth the trouble, it may be because you've never found your larger job.

Years ago, I discovered something. Perhaps you have learned it too. I can't serve myself and the Lord also. If I try to impress others with George Sweeting, I can't accomplish much for God. Only as I forget myself and get wrapped up in serving Jesus and others does anything happen that really counts.

Here's a test for you. Whose interests are you looking out for? Yours or Christ's? Essentially, Jesus said, "If you want to follow Me, go out and bury your own self-interests and get wrapped up in My interests."

Self has always been Public Enemy Number One to Christian maturity. Paul grieved that there was no one in Philippi to minister to the church there. "For I have no one like-minded," he said, "who will sincerely care for your state." Then he added the sad statement, "For all seek their own, not the things which are of Christ Jesus" (Philippians 2:20–21). So he sent Timothy to remind them of their calling.

Following Jesus is costly, yet eternally rewarding. I could have no greater wish for you than the thrill of following Him and being *faithful* to Him, for only then will you know ultimate success.

3 0

Chastened
Through Suffering

Songwriter Fanny Crosby went blind when she was six weeks old. When Fanny was suffering from a common cold and inflamed eyes, a family friend urged the use of hot poultices, which destroyed her sight.

Fanny Crosby later wrote about that difficult experience:

When this sad misfortune became known throughout our neighborhood, the unfortunate man thought it best to leave; and we never heard of him again. But I have not for a moment, in more than 85 years, felt a spark of resentment against him because I have always believed from my youth to this very moment that the good Lord, in His infinite mercy, by this means consecrated me to the work that I am still permitted to do.

While other eight- or nine-year-olds were preoccupied with jumping rope and playing tag, Fanny Crosby penned these words:

> *Oh, what a happy soul I am,*
> *Although I cannot see,*
> *I am resolved that in this world*
> *Contented I will be.*
> *How many blessings I enjoy*
> *That other people don't,*
> *To weep or sigh because I'm blind*
> *I cannot nor I won't.*

Fanny Crosby was able to accept her blindness as a gift from God. If God exempted Christians from suffering, pastors could stop preaching and laypeople could stop witnessing. Nonbelievers would flock to the church, for Christianity would be a gold-plated insurance policy of escape from pain. But that's not God's plan; no spiritual decision exempts anyone from suffering.

Some people may turn to God on that false premise, based on "promises" such as, "Beloved, I pray that you may prosper in all things and be in health, just as your soul prospers" (3 John 2). But they soon either grow disillusioned or come to understand that God doesn't promise us a rose garden. Instead, God gives us grace to survive in the brown, dried-out pasture in which we often find ourselves.

One aspect of suffering can be chastening. Revelation 3:19 states,

"As many as I love, I rebuke and chasten." Gideon, whose story is told in Judges, was chastened through suffering. God allowed the Midianites, fierce nomads who lived east of the Jordan River, to conquer His people because they had worshiped false gods.

Gideon had to thresh grain secretly in his father's winepress, a large square pit in the ground, because the Midianites would swoop down and raid the camp as soon as they saw the telltale dust of threshing.

As Gideon was threshing, the Angel of the Lord suddenly accosted him, saying, "The Lord is with you, you mighty man of valor!" (Judges 6:12). Gideon's response was much like ours might have been: "It doesn't look as if the Lord is with me! Here I am secretly beating out a harvest single-handedly. Our whole nation is hungry, humiliated, and enslaved. Not one threshing floor is in operation. The Midianites have practically wiped us out. And what's more, their false worship has invaded our land. Why, Lord? Why all this suffering?"

Many things in life make us ask why. A husband or wife may have walked out on the family; a teenager may be hooked on drugs. We've all felt the panic and depression, the sick feeling in our stomachs, the constant fear that we may not be up to the pressure.

It is interesting that the Angel of the Lord met Gideon as he was threshing grain. The Romans called the instrument used in Gideon's day to beat the grain and divide the chaff from the wheat a *tribulum* because it worked by putting pressure on the grain (*trībulāre,* "to press"). It's the source for our word *tribulation.* God often uses the pressure of tribulation to separate the chaff from the wheat in our lives, and so He was with the Israelites; with it He eliminates our selfish desires and allows our godly attributes to grow.

Through the centuries, Christians have associated suffering with chastisement. Though suffering can be the consequence of sin, at times it is God's way of bringing us back to Himself.

What did God have in mind for Gideon? His answer to Gideon's "Why?" was "Go in this might of yours, and you shall save Israel from the hand of the Midianites. Have I not sent you?" (v. 14). God said, "Gideon, you have been chosen to change the situation. You are My instrument to accomplish My work."

Gideon, like Moses before him and thousands after, was overwhelmed by the task. *Who, me?* he thought. Our situation is impossible; I can't change it. But God's answer to Gideon was simply a command to action. It was an order to get going, to get on with the job. And soon Israel experienced a supernatural victory as Gideon's army defeated the Midianite enemy.

Twice in my life the Lord allowed me to experience suffering. Looking back, those valleys were times of priceless fellowship and learning. Pain and suffering have a way of getting our attention and separating the chaff from what really matters in life.

Those times helped me learn that chastening is a sign of God's love. Since then, I have discovered that suffering is the shadow of the hand of God as He fashions me into His image.

3 1

Climbing Higher

As children, we used to sing with great enthusiasm and little understanding,

Climb, climb up sunshine mountain, faces all aglow;
Climb, climb up sunshine mountain where heavenly breezes blow.

Little did we realize to what extent life would be a rugged climb. As a young minister, I asked Harry Ironside of Chicago's Moody Church if the Christian life became easier with the passing years. "No it doesn't," he answered. "No one is safe . . . till they're home."

Though conversion occurs in a moment of repentance and faith, sanctification is a lifelong process involving a long, steep climb. Even the apostle Paul admitted that he had not yet attained (Philippians

3:12) but earnestly pressed forward to lay hold of all that God had in store for him.

The call of Jesus during His earthly ministry was never easy. He refused to gain followers under false pretenses. After His resurrection, He didn't hide His scars but openly said, "Behold My hands and My feet" (Luke 24:39).

An enthusiastic listener volunteered, "Lord, I will follow You wherever You go." Jesus answered, "Foxes have holes and birds of the air have nests, but the Son of Man has nowhere to lay His head." Another said, "Lord, let me first go and bury my father." The reply was as fast as lightning: "Let the dead bury their own dead, but you go and preach the kingdom of God." A third bargained, "Lord, I will follow You, but let me first go and bid them farewell who are at my house." Jesus dealt a crushing blow when He said, "No one, having put his hand to the plow, and looking back, is fit for the kingdom of God" (Luke 9:57–62).

Samuel Rutherford rightfully observed, "You will not be carried to heaven lying at ease on a feather bed." It's an uphill climb with frequent obstacles. So the question is, How do we climb higher?

First, there must be a *sincere desire.* If we don't want a closer relationship with God, it won't happen. This deep desire is illustrated in the life of Rachel, who prayed, "Give me children, or else I die!" (Genesis 30:1). It's the desire of Jacob, who pleaded, "I will not let You go unless You bless me!" (Genesis 32:26).

Second, our desire must be undergirded by *a full dedication to God.* Just as by faith we receive Jesus as Lord, so by faith we receive the fullness of the Holy Spirit (Acts 1:8; Ephesians 5:18). The Holy Spirit ruling and reigning in my life is the essence of climbing higher.

Third, our desire and dedication must be joined by *discipline*. Paul urged each believer to "put on the Lord Jesus" (Romans 13:14). By faith, we are to live out His purity, His wisdom, and His strength. By faith, we can lay hold of all that is ours. Then, Paul added, "Make no provision for the flesh, to fulfill its lusts." Simply put, we are not to make plans for the flesh. This twofold discipline given in Romans 13:14 is the way to climb higher. "*Put on the Lord* Jesus Christ"—and "*make no provision* for the flesh."

Caleb, though weary from eighty-five years of living, was *still climbing*. Earnestly, he prayed, "Give me this mountain." God honored his desire, dedication, and discipline—and Hebron became the inheritance of Caleb (Joshua 14:12–14).

With John Bunyan, we agree: "The hill, though high . . . I covet to ascend." As we live out Paul's instructions, we can climb higher, day by day.

Are We Responsible for Results?

Jean-François Millet's famous painting *The Sower* captures the struggle between the faithful sower scattering seed and the rapid encroachment of night. The *sower* represents all the followers of Jesus. The *seed,* according to Matthew 13, is the good news of the gospel. The *enemy* is Satan. But what about the *four types of soil?* Too often responsibility for success in sharing is placed on the sower. But are we really responsible for results?

After we profess faith in Jesus as Lord, our natural response is to proclaim the Good News from the housetop because salvation is too good to keep. However, Jesus seems to say, "Before you hurry off to be My witness, you should understand that there are four types of soil."

First, Jesus spoke about the *wayside soil.* "Some seed fell by the wayside; and the birds came and devoured them" (Matthew 13:4).

No Christian scatters seed perfectly. Some seed will fall on the wayside path regardless of our skill. These paths were common, crisscrossing the countryside. Often birds followed the sower, seeking especially the seed that fell on the wayside. What the birds didn't eat was often trampled underfoot by travelers.

The wayside hearer described in verse 19 is one who doesn't understand the message. The seed doesn't take root. It lies on the surface, exposed and unprotected. The soil is hard, dry, and unreceptive. When your witness falls upon wayside soil, don't be discouraged, but rather continue to sow the gospel faithfully. Our primary responsibility is to sow seed.

"Some fell on *stony places,* where they did not have much earth" (v. 5, italics added). Israel is a land of rocks. In many places there is limestone under the soil, though often only inches from the surface. Inevitably, some seed falls on rocky soil.

"But he who received the seed on stony places, this is he who hears the word and immediately receives it with joy," Jesus said, "yet he has no root in himself, but endures only for a while. For when tribulation or persecution arises because of the word, immediately he stumbles" (vv. 20–21).

The rocky soil person is the one who looks like the real thing in his response to the Word but has no root. He may glitter like a Fourth of July sparkler, but he burns out just as fast. Why? Verse 21 says, "He has no root." Maybe he came because of the emotion of the moment. Possibly he saw in the gospel a quick fix for broken dreams. The apostle John wrote, "They went out from us, but they were not of us" (1 John 2:19).

"And some [seed] fell among *thorns,* and the thorns sprang up and choked them" (Matthew 13:7, italics added). A better translation of the word *thorns* is "weeds," and weeds grow more easily than anything else! This describes the person who hears the Good News, but the daily cares of life choke the seed and he is unfruitful. The future looks good and there is a plant, but no fruit. This person is not a hard person, like the wayside soil. Nor is he shallow, like the rocky soil. This is the uncommitted one who wants both worlds. He wants Jesus and the world too.

Jesus described this person in verse 22: "Now he who received seed among the thorns is he who hears the word, and the cares of this world and the deceitfulness of riches choke the word, and he becomes unfruitful."

As we faithfully share the gospel, the seed will fall into these kinds of soil: wayside, rocky, and thorn infested.

But the good news is that just as there are three kinds of bad soil, so there are three kinds of good soil. Some soil is so good it yields a hundredfold. Still other soil will produce sixtyfold, while some other soil brings forth thirtyfold. The yield of the harvest depends on the quality of the soil.

All believers bear some fruit from time to time. If there's no fruit, we should examine ourselves regarding the reality of our salvation. Our primary concern is not how much fruit we bear, but our faithfulness to sow the good seed.

The point is not human ability, intelligence, or charisma, but the power of the seed of the gospel as it meets the good soil prepared by the Holy Spirit. Results are God's responsibility . . . and faithfulness is ours!

3 3

Keeping the Faith

A river without banks becomes a swamp. In the same way, faith serves as the banks that prevent a Christian's life from becoming a "spiritual swampland."

As Paul approached the end of his life, he reminded Timothy, "I have fought the good fight, I have finished the race, I have *kept the faith*" (2 Timothy 4:7, italics added).

How can we keep the faith?

To keep the faith, we must *know the faith*. The foundation of our faith is the Bible, and our faith must be well defined and clearly understood. It is difficult if not impossible to safeguard a shadow-like set of beliefs. A vague faith is hard to keep or defend. Peter reminds us to "be ready to give a defense to everyone who asks you a reason for the hope that is in you" (1 Peter 3:15).

A century ago, Benjamin Warfield wrote:

The Word of the living God is our sole assurance that there has been a redemptive work exercised by God in the world. Just in proportion as our confidence in this Word shall wane, in just that proportion shall we lose our hold upon the fact of a redemptive work of God in the world.

The faith that we are to keep is given to us in the Scriptures.

However, it's not enough to know the faith. We must *affirm the faith.* Biblical Christianity is contrary to the natural man and cannot be maintained without continual affirmation. That's why we're told to "*fight* the good fight of faith."

Not only must the faith be affirmed before the world, it must be reaffirmed *among ourselves.* Deuteronomy 6 outlines the pattern for families that can be applied to all faith keeping. Notice the fourfold instruction:

And these words which I command you today shall be in your heart; you shall *teach them* diligently to your children, and shall *talk of them* when you sit in your house, when you walk by the way, when you lie down, and when you rise up. You shall *bind them* as a sign on your hand, and they shall be as frontlets between your eyes. You shall *write them* on the doorposts of your house and on your gates. (vv. 6–9, italics added)

God's people were to *know* the faith, to *teach* the faith, to *talk* the faith, to *live* the faith, and to *write* the faith for all to see; and even after all that, they were warned, "*Beware,* lest you forget the Lord" (v. 12, italics added).

Third, we need to *undergird the faith.* It is my conviction that the faith is best undergirded by an intentional separation to Christ coupled with a separation from the world. J. B. Phillips translates Romans 12:2 with special clarity: "Don't let the world around you squeeze you into its own mould."

The New Testament word for church is *ekklesia,* which means "called-out ones." A truly Christian institution, by its very nature, is called to a superior life.

Fourth, we are to *share the faith.* An individual or institution that fails to share the faith will ultimately not keep the faith. Paul reminds us of our awesome calling: "Therefore we are ambassadors for Christ . . . : we implore you on Christ's behalf, be reconciled to God" (2 Corinthians 5:20). It is sobering to realize that God makes His appeal through you and me. That's our position! We must *share* the faith in order to *keep* the faith.

The illustrious teacher Alexander MacLaren pointed out that "Christianity is the only religion that has ever passed through periods of decadence and purified itself again. Men have gone back to the Word and laid hold again of it in its simple omnipotence, and so decadent Christianity has sprung up again into purity and power."

May the written Word of God *renew* us. May Jesus, the living Word of God, *empower* us.

Jude 24–25 (italics added) promises God's power . . . which is able to keep us from quitting:

Now to Him *who is able to keep you from stumbling,* and to present you faultless before the presence of His glory with exceeding joy, to God our

Savior, who alone is wise, be glory and majesty, dominion and power, both now and forever.

So, as we go through this day, this week, and this year, let us *"keep the faith."*

3 4

Eternal Reliability

Nothing provides a sense of security and a spirit of well-being as does God's day-by-day consistency. Of God, the Bible says, "You are the same, and Your years will have no end" (Psalm 102:27).

God is the same in His nature, attributes, and desires. He doesn't increase or decrease. He doesn't improve or deteriorate.

Malachi 3:6 states, "For I am the Lord, I do not change; therefore you are not consumed." God's reliable character enables us to keep going when we feel like quitting.

The New Testament book of James expresses God's consistency this way: "Every good gift and every perfect gift is from above, and comes down from the Father of lights, with whom there is no variation or shadow of turning" (1:17). God is eternally reliable.

The psalmist spoke continually of God's faithfulness, especially in Psalm 89: "I will sing of the mercies of the Lord forever; with my mouth will I make known Your faithfulness to all generations. . . .

Your faithfulness You shall establish in the very heavens" (vv. 1–2). Even creation affirms God's faithfulness and dependability.

Because of God's faithfulness, I can predict when the leaves of a tree change color and fall to the ground. Psalm 89 continues:

"Your faithfulness also [is found] in the congregation of the saints" (v. 5) Simply put, we reflect God's faithfulness.

"Your faithfulness . . . surrounds You" (v. 8).

"You rule the raging sea; when its waves rise, You still them" (v. 9). God is in control.

"The heavens are Yours, the earth also is Yours" (v. 11).

"The north and the south, You have created them" (v. 12).

"You have a mighty arm; strong is Your hand, and high is Your right hand" (v. 13).

"Righteousness and justice are the foundation of Your throne; mercy and truth go before Your face" (v. 14).

"Blessed are the people who know the joyful sound! They walk, O Lord, in the light of Your countenance" (v. 15).

"Our shield belongs to the Lord" (v. 18).

Yes, the Lord God is our standard of dependability and steadfastness. When everything else fails, He doesn't fail.

It is no surprise to me that the early Christians continued steadfastly in doctrine, fellowship, communion, and prayer (Acts 2:42).

A Bible verse concerning God's reliability is Lamentations 3:22–23: "Through the Lord's mercies we are not consumed, because His compassions fail not. They are new every morning; great is Your faithfulness."

How assuring it is to *always* be able to count on God. Even when everything else in life fails us, He is eternally reliable!

3 5

Thankfulness

When the Pilgrims arrived at Plymouth Colony, they believed God was with them and that His mercies were everlasting. They lived life recognizing God's sovereignty and His infinite care. This was their secret of thanksgiving, which has come to be associated so closely with them.

Thankfulness ought to be an everyday experience. It is a sign of spiritual health and should be the pulse of life. It enables us to be faithful regardless of our trials.

Consider the length and breadth of thankfulness. Under what circumstances can we be thankful? How long and how wide is our thankfulness? I'm not thinking of the "forever" quality of thankfulness, for gratitude to God will never end. In fact, our thankfulness to God will only grow as we come to understand His ways more clearly and fully.

But as to the length and breadth of our thankfulness, under what circumstances can we be thankful? The Bible tells us there are *no limits*. God's answer is expressed by two small, all-inclusive words: *always* and *all*. Scripture says we can be thankful *always* in *all* situations.

When the apostle Paul wrote his first letter to the Christians in the Greek city of Thessalonica, he was addressing those who had experienced hardships. But as he closed his letter (5:16–18), he urged three surprising actions: "Rejoice always, pray without ceasing, in everything *give thanks*" (italics added).

This suggests the staggering length and breadth of thankfulness. How can we in every circumstance rejoice, pray, and give thanks? We can do this only because God is in control. He loves us, He cares, and He acts on our behalf.

What is the height of Christian thankfulness? How thankful should we be? We should be thankful that we have God's life. We should be thankful that our sins have been forgiven and forgotten. We should be thankful that Jesus has broken the power that made us slaves to sin. Sin does not have dominion over us any longer; we have been set free and are now the children of God.

But there's more. In Colossians 1:12, Paul revealed his prayer that the Colossian Christians might give "thanks to the Father who has qualified us to be partakers of the inheritance of the saints in the light." "Thank God," he was saying, "because He has made you suitable, equipped for your role in Christ's coming kingdom of glory." He has made us ready *right now.*

No wonder the apostle John got excited: "Beloved, now we are children of God, and it has not yet been revealed what we shall be, but we know that when He is revealed, we shall be like Him, for we shall see Him as He is" (1 John 3:2). Thank God: We shall one day be like Him.

Depth is the third dimension of New Testament thankfulness. In Colossians 3:17, Paul concluded a summary of Christian life principles by writing, "And whatever you do in word or deed, do all in the name of the Lord Jesus, *giving thanks* to God the Father through Him" (italics added). Whatever you do—in word or deed, speech or action—do it in the name of the Lord Jesus Christ.

To do something in Jesus' name means to do it in His interest and for His sake. We are called to speak and act on His behalf. To what extent? "Whatever." *All.* Just as we have received an all-encompassing grace, so we are called to make *a total return.* We are to do all in the name of Jesus. All of life is really one big . . . "Thank you" to God.

A Blueprint for Life

We sometimes refer to Scripture as "God's Word" without actually stopping to consider that the Bible is literally God speaking to us. It's God's instrument to help us understand the need for personal salvation and His provision for our spiritual growth.

The Bible is a blueprint for how God's people ought to live. Therefore, a first step to understanding the Bible is making a personal commitment to Jesus as Lord. An unbeliever can read the Bible and receive considerable inspiration, but the committed Christian receives infinitely more.

Let me share some thoughts on *how to read the Bible.*

Read the Bible *prayerfully.* Prayer is the key to understanding the Bible. All of us in reading some book have, at times, wished the author were present to answer and explain some things, but that's rarely possible. Amazing as it seems, we can speak directly to the Author of the Bible. James said, "If any of you lacks wisdom, let him ask of God" (James 1:5).

God enjoys giving His children understanding. The Holy Spirit, who inspired the writers of Scripture, is also our teacher; without the guidance of the Holy Spirit, we limit our comprehension.

Second, we need to read the Bible *carefully.* Of the Christians in Berea it was said, "These were more fair-minded than those in Thessalonica, in that they received the word with all readiness" (Acts 17:11). The Bereans "searched the Scriptures daily" (v. 11). That calls for faithfulness and discipline.

As we study the words, phrases, and verses of the Bible, our spirits are fed and we grow. Martin Luther studied the Bible as one would gather apples:

First, I shake the whole tree, that the ripest might fall. Then I climb the tree and shake each limb, and then each branch and then each twig, and then I look under each leaf.

Besides reading the Bible prayerfully and carefully, we should read it *systematically.* For the best results, it's helpful to set aside a definite time and place to read the Bible.

It's best to begin at the beginning. In reading any other book, we start with chapter 1. To start a novel or biography in the middle can be confusing. The same thing holds true for the Bible. It's difficult to understand Exodus apart from Genesis, or Hebrews apart from Leviticus. There's also a danger in becoming so attached to a few favorite sections of the Bible that we neglect the very passages we really need. We need to read the Bible systematically.

It's helpful to use a notebook and list some relevant questions: Who is speaking? To whom is this written? What is the background of the writer and the receiver? What are the main ideas? What seems to be the key verse? What message is there for me today?

Finally, we should read the Bible *believingly*. "Without faith it is impossible to please [God]" (Hebrews 11:6). We read some books quite casually, but the Bible should be examined with faith and expectation.

Sometimes you hear someone say, "Look at me when I'm talking to you!" The Bible is God talking to us. And if we're paying attention, it will enable us to see Him much clearer.

3 7

Cultivate the Inner Life

These days, everyone is bombarded by distractions. Radios and television sets blare all day long. Telephones ring incessantly. Automobiles and airplanes roar by. With all this noise, it gets harder and harder to establish and maintain a *quiet* time with God. Yet that's exactly why it is so important for believers to cultivate the inner life.

Quiet time is the time set aside each day for prayer, Scripture reading, meditation, and the cultivation of the life of the Spirit. It's like a spiritual shower that cleanses, refreshes, and invigorates. It also protects us from the filth around us and fortifies us for the struggles of life. No matter who you are—new Christian, old Christian, pastor, or layperson—you have little hope of spiritual stability unless you regularly make time to develop a meaningful relationship with God.

How can we maintain a successful quiet time? Here are some suggestions.

1. *Be convinced of the importance of a quiet time.* We cannot be successful at what we do unless we are thoroughly committed to achieving it.

We believe food is necessary to our physical existence, and we eat three times a day. We must nourish the inner person for the same reason. Jesus said, "Man shall not live by bread alone, but by every word that proceeds from the mouth of God" (Matthew 4:4).

Martin Luther said, "To be a Christian without prayer is no more possible than to be alive without breathing."

2. *Cultivate a taste for communion with God.* Jeremiah wrote, "Your words were found, and I ate them, and Your word was to me the joy and rejoicing of my heart" (Jeremiah 15:16). Scripture must become part of our lives.

We should also desire to commune with God by prayer. Because I love my wife, I want to be with her. When I am traveling away from home, I look forward to calling her on the phone. If we love God, we will enjoy intimate communion with Him.

3. *Work hard to develop a quiet time.* Seek to avoid interruptions. Do not allow the telephone to rob you of your special time with God. Arrange your schedule so that you can be alone and unhurried for a specific time each day. We need to seek solitude and stillness to hear the voice of God.

I have found that people have time for just about anything that's important to them. If we want to look attractive, we spend time in front of the mirror. Civic work, even church work, takes our time because we're convinced of its importance. Yet *nothing* is more important than our time with God. If we do not maintain that time, it is not because we are too busy, but because we do not feel it is important enough.

4. *Be consistent.* Try to meet the Lord in the same place and at the same time each day.

Consistency is the important thing, but I have found that the morning hours are best for my time with God. The psalmist wrote, "My voice You shall hear in the morning, O Lord; in the morning I will direct it to You, and I will look up" (Psalm 5:3).

5. *Expect God to do something for you each day.* Pray expecting the Lord to meet a specific area in your life. Resolve not to hurry. Be still before the Lord. Ask God for a word of encouragement for *this day.*

Before long, daily quiet times will become less of an obligation and more of a source of joy. Cultivate the inner life, and you will enjoy peace, power, and perseverance!

Staying Power
Makes the Difference

Years ago I heard the story of Ali Hafed, an ancient Persian farmer with plentiful orchards, grain fields, and gardens.

One day a wise man from the East told the farmer all about diamonds and how wealthy he would be if he owned a diamond mine.

Ali Hafed went to bed that night a poor man—poor because he was discontented. Craving a mine of diamonds, he sold his farm to search for the rare stones. He traveled the world over, finally becoming so poor, broken, and defeated that he committed suicide.

One day the man who purchased Ali Hafed's farm led his camel into the garden to drink. As his camel put its nose into the brook, the man saw a flash of light from the sands of the stream. He pulled out a stone that reflected all the hues of the rainbow. The man had discovered the diamond mine of Golcanda, the most magnificent mine in all history.

Had Ali Hafed remained at home and dug in his own garden, instead of death in a strange land he would have found acres of diamonds.

It's the principle of "bloom where you're planted." Russell Herman Conwell, who made this story famous through his lecture "Acres of Diamonds," believed just that. Most of us could find acres of diamondlike opportunities in our own backyards if we would only stay in one place long enough to find them.

For many years, I traveled as an itinerant evangelist. Regardless of where I spoke—sunny California or cold Connecticut—most of the people I met were restless and discontented with their vocation and location. They were looking for "greener pastures."

Pastors often would ask if I knew of some strategic opportunity worthy of their talents. "Yes," I would answer, and then I put off giving the details of the opportunity.

In the following days, I would do everything in my power to communicate the possibilities of their present opportunities. By the end of the week, they were usually so excited about the promise of their present opportunities that they forgot to ask about the mythical, perfect church . . . somewhere else. They had learned the importance of staying power. They would bloom where they were planted.

What is staying power? Some call it perseverance. Others call it old-fashioned steadiness, faithfulness, and consistency. Today, we hear very little about hanging in till the job is done—about finishing well.

We can learn a lot about staying power by observing the characters of the New Testament church. They knew their purpose. They were guided by the words, "You shall be witnesses to Me in Jerusalem, and in all Judea and Samaria, and to the end of the earth" (Acts 1:8). They accepted this "commission" as their all-consuming, lifetime goal.

Then came their perseverance. Day after day, month after month, for years and years after Christ ascended into heaven, "they continued steadfastly in the apostles' doctrine and fellowship, in the breaking of bread, and in prayers" (2:42). They were steady, reliable, loyal, faithful, and true.

Jesus is our best example of staying power.

Repeatedly He underscored His sovereign purpose, "I must work the works of Him who sent Me" (John 9:4). After He told His disciples about His coming death, He rejected Peter's attempt to dissuade Him: "Get behind Me, Satan! You are an offense to Me, for you are not mindful of the things of God, but the things of men" (Matthew 16:23). Peter's later ministry showed he learned his lesson well.

When Jesus was on the cross, wounded and dying, He rejected the crowd's cries of "Save Yourself, and come down from the cross!" (Mark 15:30).

It takes courage to follow Jesus. It's not easy, but we, like the early Christians, can be faithful. Staying power . . . makes all the difference.

Self-Control

Alexander and his Grecian armies conquered the known world of his day. Bold and impulsive, Alexander was one of the few in history who deserved to be called "great."

Anger was not generally part of Alexander's nature. Several times in his life, however, he was tragically defeated by his temper. On one of those occasions, Cletus, a dear friend of Alexander's and a general in his army, became intoxicated and began to ridicule the emperor in front of his men. Blinded by anger, Alexander snatched a spear from a soldier and hurled it at Cletus. Although he had only intended to scare the drunken general, his spear took the life of his childhood friend.

Deep remorse followed his anger. Overcome with guilt, Alexander attempted to take his own life with the same spear, but his men stopped him. For days he lay sick, calling for Cletus and chiding himself as a murderer. Alexander the Great conquered many cities, but he failed to conquer his own spirit.

Throughout history many have destroyed their lives because they lacked self-control. The book of James offers a tried and proven remedy, "Let every man be swift to hear, slow to speak, slow to wrath" (James 1:19)

Be swift to hear. Psychotherapists tell us that *listening* is probably the most simple and effective technique for helping troubled people. Poor listening causes waste in education and industry. Thousands of marriages end each year because the husband and wife stopped listening.

James says, "Be swift to hear." Swift to hear what? Swift to hear the Word of God. The first step in conversion is hearing. The Bible tells us that "faith comes by hearing, and hearing by the word of God" (Romans 10:17). It's sad when we fail to listen to each other, but it's eternally fatal when we fail to listen to God.

Be slow to speak. Everyone seems to have something to say. Never before in history have so many said so much and done so little! Zeno, the ancient philosopher, once said, "We have two ears and one mouth; therefore, we should listen twice as much as we speak." That's good advice! Unfortunately, some people shift their minds into neutral and stomp the gas pedal of careless talk. Solomon wrote, "Whoever guards his mouth and tongue keeps his soul from troubles" (Proverbs 21:23).

Be slow to wrath. Why should we be slow to anger? James continues, "For the wrath of man does not produce the righteousness of God" (James 1:20). Human anger hinders God's work. When a per-

150

son loses his temper, he loses the ability to think soundly and make balanced decisions.

It makes a lot of sense to be swift to hear . . . slow to speak . . . and slow to wrath.

40

A Fifty-Year Partnership

My wife and I began our courtship on a toboggan run in 1940. It may have started out downhill, but it's been a wonderful climb together ever since. That outing, sponsored by our church youth group, led to a seven-year courtship and over fifty years of marriage so far.

Martha and Oswald Schnell, my wife's parents, bakers by trade, immigrated to America from Seigen, Germany, in 1922. My parents, William and Mary Sweeting of Glasgow, Scotland, came to the United States the very same year.

Our fathers fought against each other in hand-to-hand trench warfare in Belgium during World War I. Following the war, both became ardent Christians. Tired of war in Europe and discouraged by runaway inflation, both immigrated to America seeking a better life.

It was at our childhood church in Hawthorne, New Jersey, that the curlyheaded Scottish lad and the beautiful German maiden were smitten by love. It was also at this church that we were challenged to grow in our faith. On June 14, 1947, we were united in holy matrimony.

We look back with an immense thankfulness to our parents, who were committed Christians. They also inspired us by their bravery to leave loved ones and friends to seek a better life in a new land. Several key early decisions have guided us in our fifty-year partnership.

First, like our parents before us, we decided to dedicate our marriage *to the glory of God.* This decision greatly reduced our failures and shortcomings. We determined at the very start of our marriage that Jesus Christ would be the Lord of our lives. If Jesus is Lord, then selfishness and strife are replaced by God's wisdom, which, James reminds us, is "pure, then peaceable, gentle, willing to yield, full of mercy and good fruits, without partiality and without hypocrisy" (James 3:17).

Second, we decided that our marriage would be *built on the Bible.* We accepted marriage as a divine pledge to God and to each other for a lifetime. In the Garden of Eden, God said it wasn't good for man to be alone. God didn't work out a trial marriage for Adam, nor did He arrange a short-term contract. When God brought Eve to Adam, he pronounced them one flesh—till death.

In most wedding ceremonies, the permanence of marriage is still included. The husband and the wife pledge their love to each other "for better or for worse, for richer or for poorer, in joy and in sorrow, in sickness and in health, as long as we both shall live." Marriage, according to the Bible, is a sincere commitment to each other for a lifetime.

Third, we decided that our marriage would be a *partnership*. The Bible states, "'And the two shall become one flesh'; so then they are no longer two, but one flesh" (Mark 10:8). Marriage works best when there is mutual respect and mutual submission (Ephesians 5:21). This is marriage as God planned it. Peter reminded Christians in general, "All of you be submissive to one another, and be clothed with humility, for 'God resists the proud, but gives grace to the humble'" (1 Peter 5:5).

Some marry for what they can get. They come to marriage looking for gratification, security, and companionship. For the most part, these are by-products of marriage but not the primary purpose. Marriage is giving, caring, sacrificing, and sharing together. It is a physical and spiritual partnership.

My wife and I have been abundantly blessed with friends. However, at the very start of our marriage, we determined to be *each other's best earthly friend*. Looking back, it is with inexpressible gratitude and humility that we offer great thanks to God for our wonderful partnership.

4 1

I Will Build
My Church

Verbal attacks on the church appear to be popular. One accuser labeled the church as "outdated, irrelevant, and not worth a bullet to shoot it." Another described the church as "a devouring monster to be supported rather than a place to serve mankind."

Has the church had it? In every generation, some churches perform quite poorly. Even in the first century, Jesus said of the Laodicean church: "Because you are lukewarm, and neither cold nor hot, I will vomit you out of My mouth" (Revelation 3:16).

In appraising the church, it's important to remember that the church is both human and divine. The church as a *human institution* reflects all the frailties of humans. Each of us experiences moments of fervor as well as fainting, periods of saintliness and times of sinfulness. The church was never meant to be a hothouse for the exhibition of eminent saints, but rather a nursery for newborn souls, a school for spiritual education, and an armory for our training. There's no reason to expect the church to be free from human frailties.

In a very real sense the church is a reflection of each member. Perhaps the present-day criticism of the church is a form of confession. Each church member is responsible to be an asset and not a liability.

The church is also a *divine institution,* and that truth provides hope. Jesus promised, "I will build My church, and the gates of Hades shall not prevail against it" (Matthew 16:18).

It's comforting to remember the church's origin. The church belongs to Jesus, and He calls it "My church." In fact, He guarantees its future. He is the Owner and Builder, and He promises its ultimate success. There is nothing on earth or in heaven more precious to God than His church.

The church began on the day of Pentecost. The book of Acts tells how believers "gladly" received the word (Acts 2:41). They agreed with the biblical indictment of guilt and received God's salvation. They openly confessed their allegiance to Jesus Christ and were added to the church. Being added to the church was the natural result of their conversion.

The first church, as presented in Acts 2, was conceived in a "rushing mighty wind" and moved like a hurricane. In seventy years, the first Christians went over mountain peaks and tossing seas to rock the imperial city of Rome with the gospel. The postapostolic church was equally effective. In the face of bitter persecution, the church reached out to evangelize that generation.

Christians through the centuries have found it essential to fellowship together in local assemblies. The writer of Hebrews reminds us that it is a mistake to forsake "the assembling of ourselves together" (Hebrews 10:25). Martin Luther said, "To gather with God's people in united adoration of the Father is as necessary to the Christian life as prayer."

Some time ago, I suggested to a friend that he become a member of the local church where he attended. "Oh," he said, "you don't have to be a church member to be a Christian." Though I agreed with him in a technical sense, I suggested that it's also possible to cross the ocean and not use a boat, but I wouldn't recommend it because of sharks along the way. Personally, I have discovered that the church is like a giant ship that carries me through the stormy seas of life.

The church may have *many critics*—but ultimately . . . the church has *no rival!*

4 2

Remembering Father

You may call him Dad, Pop, or Papa . . . but everyone has a father. My own father was very special to me while I was growing up. He was a provider, protector, and priest for our family.

As provider, he did whatever was necessary to maintain a roof over our heads, clothing on our backs, and enough food to eat. As protector, he held the family together, carefully guiding and guarding the children. But above and beyond everything else, my father was the priest and spiritual leader of our family. On occasion, when it was necessary to discipline us, he would say, "As spiritual head of the home, and in view of a future day when I will give account of my family to God, I am responsible to discipline you."

Needless to say, his approach gained our attention, respect, and gratitude.

My memories of my father are wholesome. He was hardworking, well organized, and very serious. He never took a seminar in fatherhood, nor did he ever read a book about parenting, but by virtue of marriage, he fathered six children, and that meant guiding and leading his family.

Though my parents often read to us about God's love, they did not specifically teach us about it, but rather modeled divine love in their everyday family living.

My dad was, without doubt, the head of our home, and no one ever wanted it any other way. At times he even lost his temper, especially when we got the giggles while he read the Bible at the evening meal. Being immigrant children, we, on rare occasions, laughed at his Scottish pronunciations of certain words. His brogue could be comical.

He was punctual to a fault so that to this day I abhor tardiness.

His life was well ordered, and we were sensitive to his routine. I can still see him sitting in the same chair each night after supper, reading his "untouched newspaper." None of the six children would think of opening it until he had finished reading it.

Though he worked hard all his life, rarely taking a vacation, he never accumulated much money. Wistfully he would comment that God couldn't trust him with riches.

He was upset by waste of any form. One light was allowed to shine in any given room.

He loathed deceit in any form. His life was built on principles he refused to violate. His word was as binding and sacred as a signed legal contract

Though the memories of my brothers and sisters vary, we all agree as to his pure faith in Christ. His commitment to pass on the faith to his children was so great that he changed churches to make sure his children were exposed to a dynamic, practical application of the Scriptures.

My father taught us many things. He helped us grow up secure, healthy, and open to the will of God. He challenged us to be and give our best. He taught us submission to him and to the government, but first and foremost to God.

He taught us truthfulness and the folly of dishonesty. He urged us never to fear standing alone, so long as we were compassionate with others. He taught us that "the call of God" was the highest call in the world, and "the glory of God" was our chief motivation. He taught us that we are to be God's faithful stewards.

I'm eternally thankful to God for the memories of a father like that.

4 3

Fully Dependable

In a "Dennis the Menace" cartoon, Dennis holds up a handful of flowers and asks Mr. Wilson, "How can anything so pretty and clean come out of the dirt?"

We could ask the same question about mankind. After detailing the sinfulness of humanity, the apostle Paul describes our potential through God the Holy Spirit. Paul lists nine lasting virtues that are the result of the Holy Spirit in our lives (Galatians 5:22–23). The seventh of these virtues is *faithfulness*.

Faithfulness speaks of God's trustworthy nature. God is accessible, available, and fully dependable. He is never too busy, too preoccupied, or too tired.

In 1923, William Runyan, of the Moody Bible Institute faculty, introduced a new hymn about God's dependability to the Christian world:

"Great is Thy faithfulness," O God my Father,
There is no shadow of turning with Thee;
Thou changest not, Thy compassions, they fail not;
As Thou hast been Thou forever wilt be.

Pardon for sin and a peace that endureth,
Thy own dear presence to cheer and to guide;
Strength for today and bright hope for tomorrow,
Blessings all mine, with ten thousand beside!

"Great is Thy faithfulness!"
"Great is Thy faithfulness!"
Morning by morning new mercies I see;
All I have needed Thy hand hath provided—
"Great is Thy faithfulness," Lord, unto me!

Revelation 19:11 reminds us that faithfulness is also a characteristic of *Jesus*. One of His names is "Faithful." He is called "Faithful and True." Revelation 1:5 also describes His work and witness as faithful. We can stake our lives on God's faithfulness.

Faithful also describes His priesthood. We can fully depend on Him to bring us into God's presence (Hebrews 2:17). And, in Hebrews 3:2, the word *faithful* sums up Christ's ministry.

In the same way, God requires us to be faithful. Jesus commended the "faithful servant" in His parable of the talents. He said, "Well done, good and faithful servant" (Matthew 25:21).

Faithfulness for you and me means loyalty to Jesus and to the Bible. It also means submission to God's will. It means loving and serving in His church and caring for others.

Our awesome God is our primary example of dependability. The better I know His faithfulness, the more faithful I will be. Faithfulness is the result of the Spirit of God filling and controlling our lives.

4 4

God's Hurry

Have you ever thought of God as being "in a hurry"? Probably not. Too often we think of God as having no concern with passing time. We fortify this notion by quoting, "With the Lord one day is as a thousand years, and a thousand years as one day" (2 Peter 3:8). And yet the note of urgency runs through the entire Bible. We would do well to ask ourselves the question, "Is God *ever* in a hurry?"

During Jesus' earthly life, He gave several illustrations that convey urgency. While speaking to a crowd of religious leaders, Jesus told the story of the Prodigal Son (Luke 15). The son rebelled against his father, much like mankind has rebelled against the heavenly Father. After the prodigal wasted his possessions in "riotous living," he recognized his sins and returned to his father and home.

The father in the story represents God the Father waiting for our return. The Scripture says, "But while he was still a long way off, his father saw Him and was filled with compassion for him; he *ran* to his son, threw his arms around him and kissed him" (Luke 15:20 NIV, italics added).

J. B. Phillips translates verses 22–24: "'Hurry!' called out his father to the servants, 'fetch the best clothes and put them on him! Put a ring on his finger and shoes on his feet, and get that fatted calf and kill it, and we will have a feast and a celebration! For this is my son— he was dead, and he's alive again. He was lost, and now he's found!'" The father not only *hurried* to meet his lost son, but he hurried to give him a royal welcome.

Jesus was aware of fleeting time. On another occasion, Jesus said, "As long as it is day, we must do the work of him who sent me. Night is coming, when no one can work" (John 9:4 NIV).

Although Jesus told His disciples of His coming death and resurrection, they were still unprepared. On Resurrection morning, an angel appeared to the women and said, "He is not here; he has risen, just as he said. Come and see the place where he lay. Then *go quickly* and tell his disciples: 'He has risen from the dead'" (Matthew 28:6–7 NIV, italics added).

The message of the Resurrection required *haste*. Mary Magdalene and the other women told Peter and John, and they *ran* together to the sepulcher (John 20:4).

When Philip the evangelist was directed by God to evangelize the Ethiopian, we are told, "Philip *ran* to him" (Acts 8:30, italics added). Philip was in a hurry to do God's work.

Paul challenged each of us to make "the most of every opportunity, because the days are evil" (Ephesians 5:16 NIV). He also urged

Timothy to "fan into flame the gift of God, which is in you" (2 Timothy 1:6 NIV).

In the final book of the Bible, the call to readiness is repeated: "I am coming soon. Hold on to what you have, so that no one will take your crown" (Revelation 3:11 NIV).

J. I. Packer has this to say about urgency:

> Whatever we may believe about election, the fact remains that men and women without Christ are lost and going to hell. . . . "Except you repent," said our Lord to the crowd, "you shall all . . . perish." And we who are Christ's are sent to tell them of the One—the only One—who can save them from perishing. Is not their need urgent? . . . Does that not make evangelism a matter of urgency for us?[1]

I'm reminded of the warning of Jesus to a lukewarm church that had lost its urgency: "Because you are lukewarm—neither hot nor cold—I am about to spit you out of my mouth" (Revelation 3:16 NIV).

The greatest threat facing the church today is "lukewarmness."

I heard a fictitious story about a farmer who was awakened in the middle of the night when his alarm clock struck seventeen! Frantically, he hurried through the farm house calling, "Wake up! Wake up! It's later than it's ever been before."

Every old-time circus had a barker who promoted the various attractions. With great enthusiasm, he would call, "Hurry! Hurry! Hurry!" as the crowd flocked to the various events.

In my mind, I hear a greater voice calling, "Hurry! Hurry! Hurry! . . . For those I love die so soon." This call is not to a cheap, passing sideshow, but to the opportunity of eternal life. God's voice calls with urgency, "Stir up *your gift* . . . Redeem *the time* . . . Work *while it is day* . . . Hurry! . . . Hurry! . . . Hurry!"

NOTE

1. J. I. Packer, *Evangelism and the Sovereignty of God,* 2d ed. (Downers Grove, Ill.: InterVarsity Press, 1991), 98.

Aging Well

Thanksgiving Day has always been a favorite holiday of mine. It comes after harvest, near the end of the year, amid autumn's riotous grand finale. To me, it is a fitting symbol for graceful human aging—colorful, abundant, and satisfying.

"For the first time in human history, most people can expect to live into their 70s in reasonably good health," says the *Oxford Book of Aging,* and "those over age 85 are the fastest-growing group in our population."

Because the Christian views life as a special gift from God, we find divine purpose and potential in each decade of life. Nevertheless, there are guidelines for "growing older," just as there are guidelines for "growing up."

An attitude of gratitude is essential to aging well. The everyday, common pleasures of life—the ability to get up in the morning, the smell of fresh coffee, the taste of bacon and eggs, the sight of a robin in spring, and the fragrance of a June rose—all are cause for gratitude. The apostle Paul urges us to be "giving thanks always for all things" (Ephesians 5:20).

There's a lot that's good about aging. Aging brings increased opportunity to *remember* . . . to write those letters we have failed to write, to revive old friendships that might otherwise be forgotten. The golden years offer a freedom from hurry. I refuse to rush to an airport.

I'm also learning to savor the daily unplanned encounters, as well as to read the books on my library shelf that beg to be read. I enjoy seeking out old friends and offering a warm, heartfelt "Thank you."

Aging, at least for some, provides freedom from excessive want and a peace that comes from a simpler lifestyle.

Of course, the most precious freedom of all is the freedom Jesus spoke about: "If you abide in My word, you are My disciples indeed. And you shall know the truth, and the truth shall make you free" (John 8:31–32).

Another key to aging well is continued *personal involvement.* Each of us is a debtor (Romans 1:14). We owe the world a life. Withdrawing from responsibility can be hurtful because we lose what we do not use. I like to remind friends that getting older is like water skiing: When you *slow down,* you *go down.*

The optimism of Caleb (Numbers 13) winds my clock: "I am this day eighty-five years old . . . [Just] as my strength was then, so now is my strength for war. . . . Now . . . give me this mountain"

(Joshua 14:10–12). Caleb was obviously physically fit, which is a major help in aging well.

Aging usually reduces responsibility, but *continued involvement* is necessary for a feeling of self-worth. Paul shared his prayer: "That I may finish my race with joy" (Acts 20:24).

Aging well is closely related to the development of the inner life.

The inner person is the real me. This is the person God is primarily concerned about—not so much my image, but the inner me. Paul specifically brings this to our attention: "Even though our outward man is perishing, yet the *inward man* is being renewed day by day" (2 Corinthians 4:16, italics added). This inward person can be renewed and nurtured through prayer, meditation, reading the Scriptures, church attendance, and continued involvement in the lives of others.

Aging well is greatly enhanced by an attitude of trust in God. I find strength in the words of Isaiah: "Even to your old age, I am He. . . . *I will carry you!* I have made, and I will bear; even *I will carry*, and will deliver you" (Isaiah 46:4, italics added).

I was walking along an ocean beach with my four-year-old granddaughter, Katie. The soft sand made walking difficult, and she quickly tired. "Grandpa, will you carry me?" she asked. I hesitated, as I too found walking difficult. "If you carry me now," she said, "when you're old and little, Grandpa, I will carry you." Infused with new strength, I swept her into my arms and carried her all the way home.

Aging well is greatly helped if we remember God's promise: "I *will* carry, and *will* deliver you."

4 6

Hello, My Friend

I began broadcasting on a regular basis in 1948 with a program called *Inspiration Time.* I earnestly wanted to communicate to my listeners, so I used a conversational tone and imagined that I was speaking to a longtime acquaintance. I opened by saying, "Hello, my friend."

That phrase has appeared and reappeared in my radio scripts over the past fifty years till it has become a trademark. As I minister in many places, invariably listeners will warmly approach me with the greeting, "Hello, my friend." To this day, most of my correspondence is signed, "Your friend."

Building friends is one of life's highest privileges. God's first sentence after creating man was, "It is not good that man should be alone" (Genesis 2:18). We were created for friendship, not loneliness. Yet the reality of sin in our world not only turns us away from friendship with God, but friendship with others.

Faith in Jesus Christ not only restores a right relationship with God but enables us to experience freedom from self, resulting in a new relationship with our fellowman. Repeatedly, the Bible urges the followers of Christ to pursue friendship. Jesus commanded His followers, "Love one another; as I have loved you" (John 13:34). This divine love is our identifying characteristic and the very proof of our relationship with God (v. 35). The apostle John concluded his third letter with the statement, "Our friends greet you. Greet the friends by name" (3 John 14). Apparently, the early followers of Jesus were known as "the friends."

We encourage friendship by a spirit of acceptance. Halfhearted, conditional acceptance frustrates friendship. Upon receiving Jesus as Lord, we experienced complete acceptance by God. This unconditional acceptance is our model for accepting others. The Spirit of God replaces our cautious, calculating, conditional attitude with God's unconditional love. Paul's words excite me, "Receive one another, just as Christ also received us, to the glory of God" (Romans 15:7).

We encourage friendship by consciously seeking to be a friend. Proverbs 18:24 says, "A man who has friends must himself be friendly." We show ourselves friendly by taking the initiative in speaking to people. A pleasant smile and a cheerful word go a long way. This can be further expressed in quality listening, learning, and eventually entering into the circumstances of other lives.

We encourage friendship by exploring common interests. David and Jonathan of the Old Testament were both military men. They enjoyed common pursuits. Their friendship was broad and deep. Common interests can provide a solid building block for friendship, provided they are God honoring.

We foster friendship by making a serious commitment. Jonathan and David agreed to be special friends by verbally promising to support each other throughout life, through every trial. They even bound themselves together by an oath. There was no back door to their friendship.

Dramatically, Jonathan, the prince, shared the full and true meaning of friendship by giving to David, the shepherd boy, his robe, armor, sword, bow, and belt. He committed himself to David without reservation.

This kind of openness is probably the most difficult part of building friendships. I have wrestled with this area of complete self-disclosure to another, yet without it all friendships remain shallow.

We also encourage friendship by being generous with praise and sensitive with criticism. Add to this a good sense of humor, a double dose of patience, and a heaping tablespoon full of humility.

It is comforting and exciting to know that, because of our faith, we are fused into God's worldwide family and gain a host of friends universally. This is awesome and wonderful. However, that does not exempt us from the responsibility of cultivating "special friends." In fact, we need those good friends at every step of life to lift and enlarge our Christian life.

Life apart from quality friends is *lonely!* Remember, "A man who has friends must himself be friendly."

4 7

How to
Overcome Fear

Ever since the day Adam and Eve disobeyed God and hid in the garden, fear has plagued the human race.

Of course, not all fear is bad. We need the fear that keeps us from touching a high-voltage wire or driving through a stoplight. Above all else, we need "the fear of God," which is a sacred respect for the God who made us. Repeatedly the Scriptures remind us, "The fear of the Lord is the beginning of knowledge" (Proverbs 1:7). Three times in Psalm 103 David tells us that God's blessings are for those who fear Him. This kind of fear builds and strengthens people.

The fear that burdens is, of course, something else. It's an anxious fear that chills, freezes, and kills. God is against that kind of fear. Repeatedly, when God has spoken to men His first words have been "Fear not." The key to overcoming fear is faith—faith in God. If we fear the future, we need to cultivate faith; and if we have faith, we need not be bullied by fear.

Psychologists suggest four basic fears.

1. *Fear of want.* "What if I lose my job?" "What if I'm sick and can't work?" Are these legitimate? Surprisingly, the Bible says they are not, because God is the great Provider. Jesus said, "If God so clothes the grass of the field, which today is, and tomorrow is thrown into the oven, will He not much more clothe you . . . ? Therefore do not worry, saying, 'What shall we eat?' or 'What shall we drink?' or 'What shall we wear?'. . . For your heavenly Father knows that you need all these things" (Matthew 6:30–32).

We need to ask, is Jesus sufficient to supply my needs? Is He faithful? David said, "I have been young, and now am old; yet I have not seen the righteous forsaken, nor his descendants begging bread" (Psalm 37:25).

2. *Fear of suffering.* We fear sickness, sorrow, loneliness, and grief. God does not shield us from all suffering, for it is part of life. But He will limit and control it, and He will use it for our good.

Our suffering may be for the glory of God, the accomplishing of His purposes, or the refining of our character. Whatever the reason, we can trust the God who permits it, rest on His gracious provision, and leave the outcome in His hands.

Suffering provides opportunity to know the presence of Christ in a way we would not otherwise. That was the experience of the apostle Paul. He said in 2 Corinthians 12:8 that three times he asked God to remove his affliction, and God said no. Paul added, "And He said to me, 'My grace is sufficient for you, for My strength is made perfect in weakness.' Therefore most gladly I will rather boast in my infirmities, that the power of Christ may rest upon me" (v. 9).

God is in control of life's circumstances. When He allows suffering, He will use it for His glory and our good—and He will be with us.

3. *Fear of failure.* We are afraid of falling short in school, on the job, in social situations, or in competition. We fear failure because we rely on ourselves and usually want our desires and not His.

God is concerned with faithfulness, obedience, and character. If we set our sights on doing God's will, He will help us succeed. The roster of the heroes of faith in Hebrews 11 is made up of those who made it the business of their lives not only to believe God, but to *do His will.*

The first chapter of Joshua gives three rules for success: Go forward (v. 2), trust God (v. 7), and be guided by His Word (v. 8). God in turn promises, "I will not leave you nor forsake you" (v. 5).

4. *Fear of death.* An old song suggests that "everybody wants to go to heaven, but nobody wants to die!" The good news is that Jesus has won the victory over death, and no one who trusts in Him needs to be afraid of death. Jesus said, "Because I live, you will live also" (John 14:19).

In a fear-filled world, God offers to free us from all our fears.

4 8

The Joy of
Growing Older

One of the famous puzzles of ancient literature is the Riddle of the Sphinx: "What goes on four feet, then on two feet, and then on three? But the more feet it goes on, the weaker it be?" The answer is *man*. In childhood he creeps on all fours. As an adult he walks erect on two feet. Then in old age he steadies himself with a cane . . . a third "foot."

Life is a journey from helplessness to strength, and then, if life continues, we return to dependence again. Many people find the latter years a welcome relief, while others find trials. Most feel that old age comes too soon.

Age is a time of change and adjustments. It's a time when we lay aside our earlier occupations for leisure, personal pursuit, or at least work that is less demanding. Meanwhile, we make the inevitable discovery that our strength and our energy aren't what they used to be.

Some aspects of aging are welcome. One is release from the obligations of work. We are free to do the things that in earlier years were beyond our reach. Family fellowship becomes more rewarding as children grow and bring home the first grandchild.

However, beyond the joys, we understand that life is winding down—and nothing can be done about it.

Apart from God, growing older can be a big challenge. It's the beginning of the end brought on by sin. For those, however, who have received Jesus Christ, age has a point and purpose. It can be a time of growth, usefulness, and joyful anticipation.

In Paul's farewell to the elders of the church at Ephesus (Acts 20:24, italics added), he told them: "None of these things move me; nor do I count my life dear to myself, so that I may finish my race *with joy.*"

The latter years are a *wonderful opportunity* to fulfill God's will—*with joy!*

When Paul spoke to the Ephesian elders, he had no idea of what God's plan for him would be. But he was willing to give God a blank check. God invites each of us to do that too. We can completely trust Him for whatever He wills for us.

The unique challenge of growing older can also give God an opportunity to improve our characters. He may want to make your life the means of bringing someone to Himself. Like the burning bush that drew Moses to God in the wilderness, God may want to make your life a flame.

Growing older offers a special invitation to focus on the person of Jesus. Paul's supreme hope was not in a system or a pattern of belief, but in a person: Jesus!

Listen to him: "According to my earnest expectation . . . that in nothing I shall be ashamed, but that with all boldness, as always, so now also Christ will be magnified in my body, whether by life or by death" (Philippians 1:20). Because of faith in Jesus, Paul could see the experience of death as a triumphant entrance to eternal life . . . which the Bible states will be far, far better! Like Paul, we can completely trust God—at any age—for whatever He wills for us.

4 9

Finishing Well

Novelist Somerset Maugham tells of an Arabian merchant who sent his servant to the city of Baghdad to buy provisions. While in the marketplace, the servant saw the figure of Death, who appeared to threaten him. In panic, the servant fled to tell his master of the encounter. He begged for the use of a horse so that he could escape to the distant town of Samara.

Later that day, the merchant also visited the Baghdad marketplace. Seeing "Death" he asked, "Why did you make a threatening gesture at my servant this morning?"

Death answered, "That was not a threatening gesture, but rather a start of surprise. I was astonished to see him here in Baghdad because tonight I have an appointment with him in the far-off town of Samara." Strategize as we will, death is certain.

In earlier days people lived life with finishing in mind, whereas today death is the great unmentionable. Psychologists claim that the majority of people refuse to face death, even to the point of rejecting a yearly checkup, lest they confront their own mortality.

People face death differently. One dies in confidence, while another dies in doubt. Some die rejoicing, while others experience remorse. Some die right, and some wrong.

It was said that when King Jehoram of Judah died, "He departed *with no one's regret*" (2 Chronicles 21:20 NASB, italics added). He died wrong because he lived wrong. However, the Scripture says of Abijah that at his death "all Israel mourned for him" (1 Kings 14:18). In spite of heredity and environment, Abijah died right.

Two descriptive words regarding death appear in 2 Peter and Philippians. In 2 Peter 1:15, the term translated "decease" in the NKJV is the Greek word *exodus,* the title of the second book of the Bible. It means "the road out." Death for the Christian is a triumphant exodus —very much like the children of Israel's release from the slavery of Egypt.

In Philippians 1:23, the apostle Paul says: "Having a desire to depart and be with Christ, which is far better." Here the Greek word is *depart,* which means "to loose." This pictures an anchor being lifted, freeing the boat to sail beyond the confines of a particular location. For the followers of Jesus death is literally an "anchors away."

Author Malcolm Muggeridge speaks of death with anticipation: "So, like a prisoner awaiting his release, like a school-boy when the end of the term is near, like a migrant bird ready to fly south, like a person in the hospital anxiously scanning the doctor's face to see whether a discharge may be expected, I long to be gone. . . . Such is the prospect of death."

John Bunyan, in his book *Pilgrim's Progress,* tells of Mr. Fearing, who dreaded death all his life and likened it to the crossing of the Jordan River by the children of Israel. However, when Mr. Fearing reached the river, the waters were at a record low and he crossed over "not much above wet-shod."

J. I. Packer reminds us, "Dying well is one of the good works to which Christians are called, and He will enable us who serve Him, *to die well.*"

The real secret of finishing well is found in living well and treating each day a special gift from God.

5 0

God Is No Quitter

Some years ago I visited Cecil B. Day Sr., the visionary founder of Day's Inn of America. Knowing the daily struggles of operating a nationwide motel chain, he chose only one picture for the wall in his office. It was the picture of a cat with bulging eyes, desperately hanging onto a clothesline, bearing the caption, "Hang in there, baby." Cecil Day had experienced thousands of reasons to quit . . . but he hung in there.

Sometimes we face temporary setbacks, but they need not lead to ultimate quitting. The biblical example of John Mark proves it is possible to quit and then recommit to your calling. You might remember that he traveled on the first missionary journey with Barnabas and Paul. Not far into the trip, he quit and went back home to Jerusalem (Acts 13:13).

As Paul and Barnabas were planning a second journey, Barnabas again wanted to take John Mark along, but Paul refused to have him. They disagreed so severely that Paul and Barnabas agreed to go their separate ways (Acts 15:37–40). Barnabas continued to work with John Mark, who eventually became dependable and even profitable to Paul (Colossians 4:10; 2 Timothy 4:11). In fact, Mark went on to write the second gospel. The "quitter" became the "finisher."

Paul reminds each Christian that those whom God "foreknew, He also predestined to be conformed to the image of His Son" (Romans 8:29). That is God's plan for each of His children. Paul also told the leaders of the church of Ephesus that his life's purpose was to "finish the race and complete the task the Lord Jesus has given me" (Acts 20:24 NIV).

Writing to the Christians in the city of Philippi, Paul reminded them that God is no quitter: "Being confident of this very thing, that He who has begun a good work in you *will complete it* until the day of Jesus Christ" (Philippians 1:6, italics added). God promises to continue the work that He has begun until it is completed.

It is an awesome thought to consider that whatever God begins, He finishes. Life is never over till it's over. And because *God* is no quitter, it's always . . . *too soon* . . . for you and me . . . *to quit!*